Workshop on Automatic Summarization for Creative Writing 2022

Gyeongju, South Korea
17 October 2022

ISBN: 978-1-7138-9106-2

Printed from e-media with permission by:

Curran Associates, Inc.
57 Morehouse Lane
Red Hook, NY 12571

Some format issues inherent in the e-media version may also appear in this print version.

Printed with permission by Curran Associates, Inc. (2024)

For permission requests, please contact the Association for Computational Linguistics at the address below.

Association for Computational Linguistics
209 N. Eighth Street
Stroudsburg, Pennsylvania 18360

Phone: 1-570-476-8006
Fax: 1-570-476-0860

acl@aclweb.org

Additional copies of this publication are available from:

Curran Associates, Inc.
57 Morehouse Lane
Red Hook, NY 12571 USA
Phone: 845-758-0400
Fax: 845-758-2633
Email: curran@proceedings.com
Web: www.proceedings.com

COLING 2022
Volume 29 (2022), No. 6

Proceedings of The Workshop on Automatic Summarization for Creative Writing

The 29th International Conference on Computational Linguistics

October 17, 2022
Gyeongju, Republic of Korea

ISSN 2951-2093

Preface

In recent years, automatic text summarization has seen dramatic advances due to the development of large neural language models such as BERT, BART, and PALM. However, the majority of work in this field focuses on the domain of single-document news summarization, given the availability of datasets such as CNN/DailyMail, XSum, NewsRoom, and NYTimes, among others. While this domain is important, it suffers from several limitations in its short input lengths, its focus on literal language, and its constrained discourse structure. While efforts in multi-document summarization of news and dialog bring in additional complexity, they do not address the larger problem of building datasets for truly challenging datasets. We envision that in the near future, summarization systems will need to be equipped with the ability to:

- Process long input sequences spanning up to hundreds of pages of text
- Analyze complex discourse structure such as narrative and multi-party dialog
- Interpret figurative language and convey the salient points in the input

An equally important yet underexplored domain for text summarization is creative writing, which includes documents such as books, stories, as well as scripts from plays, TV shows, and movies. Documents in this domain are uniquely characterized by their substantial input lengths, non-trivial temporal dependencies (e.g., parallel plot threads), complex structures which often combine narrative and multi-party dialogues, and a wide variety of styles. Successfully summarizing such texts requires making literary interpretations, conveying implicit information, and heavily paraphrasing the inputs. The challenges of creative writing summarization, then, require the development of systems that utilize techniques not yet explored in the field.

This workshop aims to bring together researchers and promote exciting work in the domain of creative writing summarization, with the hope of contributing to the next generation of summarization systems. The workshop includes papers on topics required for summarizing creative text as well as papers reporting on a shared task on creative text, encompassing four sub-tasks: summarization of chapters from novels, summarization of movie scripts, summarization of prime time television transcripts, and summarization of daytime soap opera transcripts.

In addition to the published papers, the workshop features eight invited talks from researchers working in summarization: Mirella Lapata (University of Edinburgh), Asli Celikyilmaz (Meta AI), Shashi Narayan (Google AI), Greg Durrett (University of Texas, Austin), Mohit Bansal (University of North Carolina, Chapel Hill), Miguel Ballesteros (Amazon AI Labs), Lu Wang (University of Michigan), and Xiaojun Wan (Peking University).

We invite you to enjoy the workshop talks and the proceedings!

The Organizing Committee

Organizing Committee

Kathleen McKeown (Columbia University), chair
Divyansh Agarwal (Salesforce Research)
Alexander Fabbri (Salesforce Research)
Simeng Han (Yale University)
Wojciech Kryściński (Salesforce Research)
Faisal Ladhak (Columbia University)
Bryan Li (University of Pennsylvania)
Ramesh Nallapati (Amazon AI Labs)
Dragomir Radev (Yale University)
Sam Wiseman (Duke University)
Tianyi Zhang (Stanford University)

Table of Contents

IDN-Sum: A New Dataset for Interactive Digital Narrative Extractive Text Summarisation
Ashwathy T. Revi, Stuart E. Middleton and David E. Millard 1

Summarization of Long Input Texts Using Multi-Layer Neural Network
Niladri Chatterjee, Aadyant Khatri and Raksha Agarwal 13

COLING 2022 Shared Task: LED Finteuning and Recursive Summary Generation for Automatic Summarization of Chapters from Novels
Prerna Kashyap 19

TEAM UFAL @ CreativeSumm 2022: BART and SamSum based few-shot approach for creative Summarization
Rishu Kumar and Rudolf Rosa 24

Long Input Dialogue Summarization with Sketch Supervision for Summarization of Primetime Television Transcripts
Nataliia Kees, Thien Nguyen, Tobias Eder and Georg Groh 29

AMRTVSumm: AMR-augmented Hierarchical Network for TV Transcript Summarization
Yilun Hua, Zhaoyuan Deng and Zhijie Xu 36

Automatic Summarization for Creative Writing: BART based Pipeline Method for Generating Summary of Movie Scripts
Aditya Upadhyay, Nidhir Bhavsar, Aakash Bhatnagar, Muskaan Singh and Petr Motlicek 44

The CreativeSumm 2022 Shared Task: A Two-Stage Summarization Model using Scene Attributes
Eunchong Kim, Taewoo Yoo, Gunhee Cho, Suyoung Bae and Yun-Gyung Cheong 51

Two-Stage Movie Script Summarization: An Efficient Method For Low-Resource Long Document Summarization
Dongqi Pu, Xudong Hong, Pin-Jie Lin, Ernie Chang and Vera Demberg 57

CREATIVESUMM: Shared Task on Automatic Summarization for Creative Writing
Divyansh Agarwal, Alexander R. Fabbri, Simeng Han, Wojciech Kryscinski, Faisal Ladhak, Bryan Li, Kathleen McKeown, Dragomir Radev, Tianyi Zhang and Sam Wiseman 67

Conference Program

October 17th, 2022

09:00–10:30 Session 1

09:00–09:30 *Modeling and Evaluating Faithful Generation across Modalities*
Mohit Bansal

09:30–10:00 *Controllable Content Creation With Planning*
Shashi Narayan

10:00–10:20 *IDN-Sum: A New Dataset for Interactive Digital Narrative Extractive Text Summarisation*
Ashwathy T. Revi, Stuart E. Middleton and David E. Millard

10:50–12:30 Session 2

10:50–11:20 *Where did I read that? It was in a book. Challenges in Summarization of Book Chapters and Dialogues*
Miguel Ballesteros

11:20–11:50 *Long Document Summarization using Efficient Attentions and Document Structure*
Lu Wang

11:50–12:10 *Summarization of Long Input Texts Using Multi-Layer Neural Network*
Niladri Chatterjee, Aadyant Khatri and Raksha Agarwal

12:10–12:30 *COLING 2022 Shared Task: LED Finteuning and Recursive Summary Generation for Automatic Summarization of Chapters from Novels*
Prerna Kashyap

October 17th, 2022 (continued)

13:50–15:40 Session 3

13:50–14:20 *Hierarchical 3D Adapters for Long Video-to-text Summarization*
Mirella Lapata

14:20–14:40 *TEAM UFAL @ CreativeSumm 2022: BART and SamSun based few-shot approach for creative Summarization*
Rishu Kumar and Rudolf Rosa

14:40–15:00 *Long Input Dialogue Summarization with Sketch Supervision for Summarization of Primetime Television Transcripts*
Nataliia Kees, Thien Nguyen, Tobias Eder and Georg Groh

15:00–15:20 *AMRTVSumm: AMR-augmented Hierarchical Network for TV Transcript Summarization*
Yilun Hua, Zhaoyuan Deng and Zhijie Xu

15:20–15:40 *Automatic Summarization for Creative Writing: BART based Pipeline Method for Generating Summary of Movie Scripts*
Aditya Upadhyay, Nidhir Bhavsar, Aakash Bhatnagar, Muskaan Singh and Petr Motlicek

16:00–18:10 Session 4

16:00–16:30 *Towards Figurative Language Generation*
Xiajun Wan

16:30–17:00 *Discourse Aware Text Summarization*
Asli Celikyilmaz

17:00–17:20 *The CreativeSumm 2022 Shared Task: A Two-Stage Summarization Model using Scene Attributes*
Eunchong Kim, Taewoo Yoo, Gunhee Cho, Suyoung Bae and Yun-Gyung Cheong

17:20–17:40 *Two-Stage Movie Script Summarization: An Efficient Method For Low-Resource Long Document Summarization*
Dongqi Pu, Xudong Hong, Pin-Jie Lin, Ernie Chang and Vera Demberg

17:40–18:10 *Summarizing Narratives with GPT-3: Measuring the next 5 years of progress*
Greg Durrett

October 17th, 2022 (continued)

IDN-Sum: A New Dataset for Interactive Digital Narrative Extractive Text Summarisation

Ashwathy T Revi and **Stuart E. Middleton** and **David E. Millard**
University of Southampton
University Rd, Highfield, Southampton SO17 1BJ

Abstract

Summarizing Interactive Digital Narratives (IDN) presents some unique challenges to existing text summarization models especially around capturing interactive elements in addition to important plot points. In this paper we describe the first IDN dataset (IDN-Sum) designed specifically for training and testing IDN text summarization algorithms. Our dataset is generated using random playthroughs of 8 IDN episodes, taken from 2 different IDN games, and consists of 10,000 documents. Playthrough documents are annotated through automatic alignment with fan-sourced summaries using a commonly used alignment algorithm. We also report and discuss results from experiments applying common baseline extractive text summarization algorithms to this dataset. Qualitative analysis of the results reveal shortcomings in common annotation approaches and evaluation methods when applied to narrative and interactive narrative datasets. The dataset is released as open source for future researchers to train and test their own approaches for IDN text.

1 Introduction

Automatic summarization has often been been studied for domains such as news and scientific reports. While there is some work on narratives like movies and books, there is limited work surrounding automatic summarization of interactive and game narratives. Extrapolating IDN performance from news article summarization results is non trivial due to longer texts and the existence of elements like characters and plot. IDN also differs from movies and books due to the presence of interactivity and game elements that make summarisation of IDN different to that of general text and/or linear narratives. Unlike novel/movie summarization, IDN has the concept of choices, structure and multiple plot lines which also affect the relative importance of sentences. Additionally, IDN text formats vary significantly and can look like novels, movie scripts, gameplay logs, or a mixture of all three.

The IDN-Sum dataset is generated from fan made transcripts of two narrative games, both sourced from Fandom[1] - *Before the Storm* published by Square Enix and *Wolf Among Us* published by TellTale Games. Different simulated playthroughs through the game are generated by implementing a ReaderBot like the one described in (Millard et al., 2018), assuming a different combination of choices for each playthrough. While these two sources account for only one type of IDN (narratives in the form of a Gauntlet, see section 3.1), it takes a step towards increasing resources available for research in this area. An analysis of dataset characteristics and performance of some baseline summarisation methods on this dataset is presented. Novel contributions of this paper are (a) a new text summarization dataset for IDN (IDN-Sum), with abstractive summaries for overall IDN and aligned extractive summaries for multiple IDN playthroughs, and (b) baseline evaluation of standard benchmarks on IDN-Sum and qualitative analysis of the predictions made by them.

2 Related Work

Most text summarization work is targeted at news, academic papers and reviews. The most commonly used summarisation dataset is the CNN/DailyMail dataset which is a collection of news articles and human written summaries (Hermann et al., 2015; Nallapati et al., 2016). Summarisation datasets for narratives include datasets with novel chapters and corresponding human written summaries from online guides, (Chaudhury et al., 2019) (Ladhak et al., 2020), extractive summaries that read like telegraphs(Malireddy et al., 2018), stories and summaries from Wattpad(Zhang et al., 2019a), transcripts and summaries of movies(Gorinski and Lapata, 2015), transcripts of TV shows (Papalampidi

[1] www.fandom.com

Proceedings of the 58th Annual Meeting of the Association for Computational Linguistics, pages 1–12
July 5–10, 2020.
https://doi.org/10.26615/978-954-452-056-4_001

et al., 2020; Chen et al., 2021) and subtitles (Aparício et al., 2016). Papers on game summarisation are few and usually involve game logs from online games like *DOTA* (Barot et al., 2021; Cheong et al., 2008) or commentary from sports(Sandesh and Srinivasa, 2017). However, IDN text is typically more similar to movie scripts or novels than game logs. The critical role dataset (Rameshkumar and Bailey, 2020) is a dataset of transcripts and summaries from critial role episodes. This is a transcript of several voice actors playing a Table top role playing game and hence captures only one playthrough of a narrative. To the best of our knowledge, IDN-Sum is the first dataset for IDN that captures multiple playthroughs of an IDN.

Unsupervised methods for automatic extractive summarisation use several methods to determine the importance of sentences including statistical methods using features like sentence position and TF-IDF, concept based methods that use external databases like WordNet, topic based methods to infer important topics, graph based methods that build intermediate graphs computed through metrics like semantic similarity, semantic methods using techniques like semantic role annotation, optimization methods that involve optimising for constraints (like maximising coverage or minimising redundancy) and fuzzy logic based methods (El-Kassas et al., 2021). Supervised methods include different RNNs and Tranformers, using pretrained models such as Bert for summarisation (Mridha et al., 2021; Liu, 2019). Variations of BertSum(Liu, 2019), SummaRuNNer(Nallapati et al., 2017), MatchSum(Zhong et al., 2020), Discobert(Xu et al., 2020), HiBert(Zhang et al., 2019b), Banditsum(Dong et al., 2018) and neusum(Zhou et al., 2018) are among the most commonly used baselines for extractive summarisation in the past three years. However, most of these were designed for short documents (CNN/DM). Longformer(Beltagy et al., 2020) is an adpatation of BertSum for longer documents. There are also summarisation approaches that are specific to the narrative domain (Gorinski and Lapata, 2015; Tran et al., 2017; Papalampidi et al., 2020).

3 IDN Dataset

3.1 Methodology for Dataset Creation

The IDN-Sum dataset consists of several simulated playthroughs through two narrative games - *Before the Storm* and *Wolf Among Us*. Both of these are narrative games in which the choices made by the player change how they experience the story. Playthroughs are simulated by assuming a different combination of choices each time. The script that generates these playthroughs is referred to as ReaderBot in this paper, following terminology used in (Millard et al., 2018). Both of these have what are referred to as a Gauntlet structure (Rezk and Haahr, 2020) which means the story changes based on player choices but then eventually all paths converge back onto a common storyline making a gauntlet shape. While this is not the only type of IDN, they were chosen based on availability of resources and smallest variation in domain from existing work.

Fan made transcripts and summaries are scraped from Fandom. The transcripts on Fandom contains the script of the game and tabs showing how the dialogue changes based on different options the player might chose throughout the game. This html page is parsed and different playthroughs are then generated by a ReaderBot(Millard et al., 2018) by choosing different combinations of options for each scene. Fandom much like Wikipedia, is a major community site with more than 31 million registered users[2]. Through the authors' own inspection, the summaries were found to be of good quality. The limitations of the ReaderBot, details of implementation and the game mechanics that are supported are described on the Github page[3].

There is only one human authored abstractive summary per episode. We take this overall abstractive plot summary from Fandom and produce extractive summaries for each playthrough using the TransformerSum[4] library. This library follows the method used in (Nallapati et al., 2017) to convert abstractive summaries to extractive summaries by greedily selecting extracts that maximise the ROUGE score with the abstractive summary until the sentence limit is hit or ROUGE score cannot be improved. Summaries were generated with target lengths of 3 (similar to CNN/DM) but also longer target lengths of 9 and 27, since for narrative datasets the source text and reference summaries are much longer. For IDN and CRD3, we also generate target length of 81 since the reference summaries for the these datasets are considerably larger than 27. The human authored abstractive summary

[2]stats taken from https://community.fandom.com/wiki/Special:Statistics

[3]https://github.com/AshwathyTR/IDN-Sum

[4]https://github.com/HHousen/TransformerSum

for each episode is also provided along with the dataset so that annotations can be generated using any alignment algorithm.

3.2 Dataset Characteristics and Comparison

Property	CNN DM	Novel	CRD3	SB	IDN
#docs	280K	4366	159	850	10K
#sents	10M	630K	524K	2M	26K
doc length	40	278	2400	2797	2290
ref length	3.8	24	141	34	72
tokens/sent	21	24	18	11	10
vocab size	681K	115K	53K	202K	10K

Table 1: Dataset Metrics: number of instances in dataset (#docs), number of unique sentences (#sents), average number of sentences in source text (doc length) and human authored reference summary (ref length), average number of tokens per sentence (tokens/sent) and number of words in vocabulary (vocab size) for each dataset

Table 1 compares **IDN-Sum (IDN)** with several other narrative datasets. The Novel Chapter dataset from (Ladhak et al., 2020) is included since it contains narrative elements like plot but is not as structurally different from the CNN/DM as the screenplay datasets. **Scriptbase (SB)**(Gorinski and Lapata, 2015) was chosen for comparison because the IDN text that is generated by the ReaderBot is very similar to screenplays. **Critical Role Dataset (CRD3)**(Rameshkumar and Bailey, 2020) was chosen since this is an example of a kind of interactive narrative, even though it does not show alternate storylines that are possible through the story world. The metrics for CNN/DM (Hermann et al., 2015; Nallapati et al., 2016) dataset is also shown for comparison since this is a widely used dataset by the NLP community for text summarisation. IDN, SB and CRD3 datasets are structured like screenplays so they were preprocessed into a format that captures the structure for consistency. The tag ':SC:' was used to separate scenes, '[EX]' was used to denote beginnings and ends of extracts and 'S0:' was used to denote non dialogue sentences (narration).

As can be observed from the table, CNN/DM has a lot more datapoints than the narrative datasets. The narrative datasets are much longer (refer length of source column). ScriptBase and IDN tend to have shorter sentences than the other datasets. The extractive summaries were generated using the alignment technique described in the last section

Dataset	no filter	stop filter
CNN/DM_3	0.56	0.56
Novel_3	0.31	0.19
Novel_9	0.44	0.29
Novel_27	0.50	0.35
CRD3_3	0.19	0.18
CRD3_9	0.34	0.31
CRD3_27	0.49	0.44
CRD3_81	0.62	0.55
SB_3	0.17	0.09
SB_9	0.3	0.18
SB_27	0.45	0.31
IDN_3	0.08	0.06
IDN_9	0.18	0.14
IDN_27	0.36	0.31
IDN_81	0.56	0.49

Table 2: ROUGE1 F1 scores of automatically aligned extractive summaries (oracle) against human authored abstractive summaries with and without stop words. Target lens 9, 27 and 81 for CNN/DM and 81 for Novel and SB was not generated since these target lengths are much greater than the average length of human written abstractive reference summaries

for target lengths 3, 9, 27 and 81 depending on the average length of the reference summaries (9, 27 and 81 was not run for CNN/DM and 81 was not run for Novel and SB datasets). The ROUGE1 F1 scores of the generated summary against the human written summary are shown in table 2. IDN has lower unique sentences and vocab size because unlike other datasets, the IDN dataset has a lot of overlap in text between datapoints since it contains hundreds of playthroughs of each episode. Since it follows the gauntlet structure, both in *Before the Storm* and *Wolf Among Us* a major portion of the story is present in all branches. This is illustrated in figures 1 and 2. Fig 1 shows the amount of token overlap between one data point in the IDN dataset with all the other data points. A similar graph showing variation in the aligned extractive summaries is also shown. As can be seen in the figure, a set of other data points have high overlap. These are other playthroughs of the same episode where only some parts of the text are different. For comparison, a similar graph is shown from ScriptBase which contains screenplays that are entirely unrelated to each other in fig 2. In this case, all data points have only a small overlap. Examples of the data are shown in Appendix A.

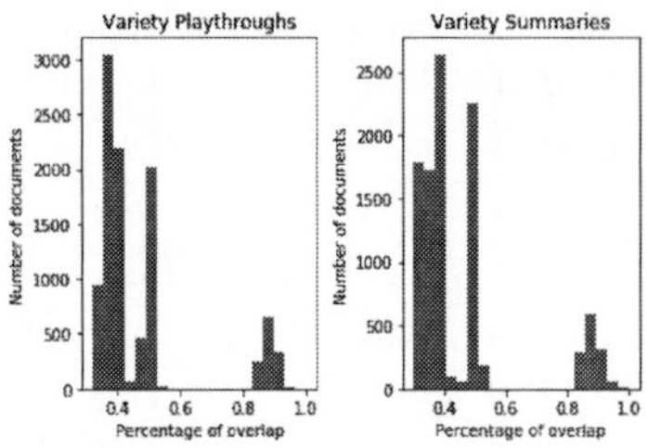

Figure 1: Variety in IDN Dataset

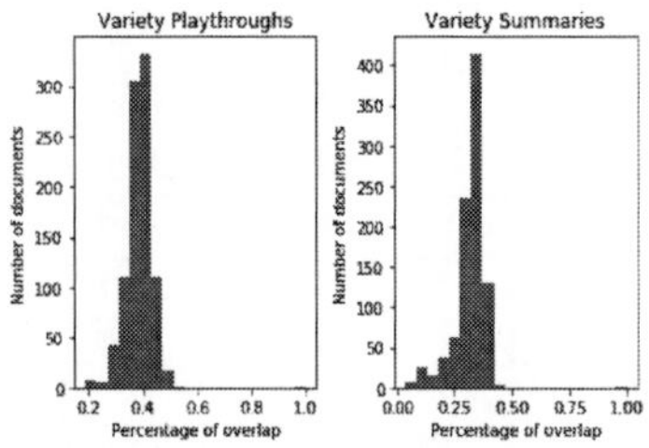

Figure 2: Variety in Scriptbase Dataset

4 Baseline Experiments

4.1 Methods

Baseline models used in this paper represent a good coverage of standard methods used for extractive text summarisation today. The baselines were chosen so that they include two simple baselines, Random-N and LEAD-N, a commonly used unsupervised method, TextRank (Mihalcea and Tarau, 2004) and two neural network based methods (transformer based approaches BertSum(Liu, 2019), Longformer(Beltagy et al., 2020) and an RNN based sequence model, SummaRuNNer(Nallapati et al., 2017)). Out of the popular baselines mentioned in section 2, SummaRuNNer was chosen because it was the most easily extendable to longer documents. BertSum was included since this was the most popular baseline and variation of it for longer documents, Longformer was included so that a more recent model is also included as a baseline. Narrative summarisation models mentioned in section 2 work at a scene level and hence return huge summaries for complete narratives/IDN's, so these methods are not included.

Random-N selects a random N sentences as the summary and Lead-N selects the first N sentences of the source text as its summary where N for each dataset is set to summary lengths 3,9,27 and 81. TextRank is similar to Google's PageRank(Page et al., 1999) algorithm where each sentence is considered in place of web pages. A sentence similarity graph is computed and used to calculate importance of sentences which are then ranked accordingly. For supervised methods, training data for extractive summarisation is generated by automatically aligning abstractive summaries with the original text by greedily maximising ROUGE scores as in (Nallapati et al., 2017). Both in case of BertSum and SummaRuNNer extractive summarisation is framed as a sequence classification task where text is first split into segments (sentences, in this case) and then each sentence is sequentially classified as either belonging to the summary or not. SummaRuNNer uses a GRU-RNN based architecture for this. We report results on two variations of Summarunner - one with default document truncation at default 100 sentences (SR) and one with document truncation changed to 3000 sentences (SRL) for narrative datasets that are long. BertSum takes a transformer based pretrained Bert model and fine-tunes it for summarisation tasks. However, it is only able to handle 512 tokens as input. Since, all of the narrative datasets are much bigger than this, we report results on LongFormer for these as well. Longformer modifies this approach for longer documents using windowed attention. While there is still a limitation on the number of tokens it can take as input, it improves on BertSum by allowing longer input sequences. Since more recent models like MatchSum and DiscoBert uses an underlying Bert model, they suffer from this limitation as well and hence, were not included as baselines.

4.2 Experiment Setup

We use gensim[5] library's implementation of the TextRank algorithm. For BertSum, we use TransformerSum library's[6] implementation of BertSum and LongFormer. At the time of running experiments, this implementation of LongFormer supported upto 4096 tokens as input. SummaRuNNer uses implementation from hpzao [7]. First 3 episodes of Wolf among us was used as training set , last 2 episodes of Wolf Among Us was used as validation and Before the storm was used as test set. Using a different game for the test ensures that there is no data leakage into the test set. Both models were trained with default parameters (except for max_epochs in TransformerSum's BertSum implementation which was set to 10 epochs rather the the default 100). Summarunner was originally

[5]https://pypi.org/project/gensim/

[6]https://github.com/HHousen/TransformerSum

[7]https://github.com/hpzhao/SummaRuNNer

Dataset_ Length	RAND-N	LEAD-N	TextRank (TR)	BertSum (BS)	SummaRuNNer (SR)	LongFormer (LF)	SummaRuNNer Long(SRL)
CnnDm_3	0.29	0.4	0.35	0.4	0.35	N/A	N/A
Novel_3	0.15	0.18	**0.26**	0.17	**0.26**	0.16	**0.26**
Novel_9	0.28	0.29	0.34	0.28	0.33	0.3	**0.35**
Novel_27	0.33	0.31	0.31	0.33	0.35	0.32	**0.36**
CRD3_3	0.02	0.03	0.08	0.03	0.03	0.02	**0.17**
CRD3_9	0.07	0.09	0.16	0.06	0.07	0.06	**0.31**
CRD3_27	0.17	0.18	0.27	0.14	0.18	0.27	**0.4**
CRD3_81	0.3	0.31	0.35	0.15	0.27	0.36	**0.47**
SB_3	0.05	0.05	0.12	0.05	0.1	0.07	**0.14**
SB_9	0.12	0.13	0.22	0.1	0.18	0.16	**0.27**
SB_27	0.24	0.23	0.32	0.21	0.27	0.27	**0.36**
IDN_3	0.02	0.04	0.04	0.008	0.04	0.04	**0.06**
IDN_9	0.06	0.09	0.1	0.05	0.11	0.08	**0.13**
IDN_27	0.17	0.17	0.24	0.12	0.2	0.2	**0.29**
IDN_81	0.35	0.32	0.4	0.16	0.27	0.31	**0.42**

Table 3: ROUGE1 F1 scores against human authored abstractive summary. SummaRuNNer (long) performs best overall. Note that Longformer (LF) and Summarunner (long) were not run for CNN/DM since these are meant for long documents and CNN/DM documents are short.

truncates documents at 100 sentences. We report performance of this model for this default case (SR) and a variation where it accepts longer documents with truncation at 3000 sentences(SRL) for narrative datasets since they are longer. In the long version, batch size had to be reduced to 1 to fit GPU memory. Each summarisation method was run with target length 3 for each dataset. Narrative datasets were also run with target lengths 9 and 27 since they have longer source documents and reference summaries. IDN and CRD3 were also run with target length 81 since reference summaries are much larger than 27 for these datasets.

4.3 Evaluation

The trained models were used to make predictions on the test set and ROUGE scores for all models were evaluated using the evaluation script from SummaRuNNer for consistency. The option setting the limit to the first x bytes was removed. This script uses the pyROUGE library[8]. ROUGE1 F1 score is calculated against the human authored abstractive summary with porter stemming (as commonly done in papers such as (Agarwal et al., 2018)) for all models and datasets and is compared in Table 3.ROUGE2 F1 scores are shown in the Appendix C. Scores against aligned extractive reference summaries can be found in Appendix B. The best and worst summaries (according to ROUGE) from the best model were also analysed qualitatively. The qualitative investigations help assess aspects of quality that are not captured by the ROUGE scores.

[8]https://pypi.org/project/pyROUGE/

5 Results

Table 3 shows the performance of the baseline models. SummaRunner scales for longer documents and the long version (SRL) outperforms the other models in all cases. Another observation is that even though the narrative datasets are considerably smaller than CNN/DM, the use of pretrained language models does not seem to be helping. While Longformer improves on performance of BertSum in many cases, it does not significantly outperform the truncated version of SummaRunner. In many cases, truncated version of SummaRunner even performs better in terms of ROUGE scores in spite of only having access to the first 100 sentences of the text, whereas Longformer has access to significantly more (4096 tokens is between 200 and 400 sentences). Average sentence lengths for each of the datasets can be seen in Table 1. A manual inspection of sample summaries was performed and the results of this analysis are discussed below.

5.1 Quality of aligned extractive summaries

The ROUGE1 F1 scores of the automatically aligned extractive summary overlap to human authored summary is shown in table 2. The ROUGE1 F1 for the narrative datasets at higher target lengths (27, 81) are comparable to that of CNN/DM at target length 3, which reflects the need for longer summaries to capture important information for longer narratives. Manual inspection of the original text and reference summaries also suggest that if all information in the human authored abstractive summary is considered equally important, it is hard to find sentence level extracts from the original text that cover all the information in case of smaller target lengths, especially for SB, CRD3 and IDN.

ROUGE F1 degrades from Novel to CRD3 to SB to IDN, especially for lower target lengths. To understand this further, the best and the worst summaries for each of the datasets were examined manually. This revealed that since words aren't weighted, many irrelevant sentences are picked up due to matching on common words (like character names) and stop words. ROUGE1 F1 scores for each of these datasets computed with the remove stopwords argument is also shown in Table 2 under 'stop filter'. The ROUGE scores of the narrative datasets degrade significantly compared to CNN/DM which stays approximately the same. This indicates the necessity of using weighted versions of ROUGE for alignment of narrative datasets, supporting findings from (Ladhak et al., 2020). It also shows CRD3 and Novel having higher scores when compared to SB and IDN. This can be traced to the presence of a few quotes from the original text in the human authored abstractive summaries for some instances in the Novel and CRD3 datasets. Since there is limited paraphrasing in these sentences, they get picked up and get higher ROUGE scores, but since there are only a few of these kinds of sentences, these datasets only have this advantage at lower target lengths.

It was also observed that summaries for SB had many sentences that are too short or are not coherent without context. Due to the presence of narration-like sentences in the Novel and IDN datasets, the overall readability of the summary was better at lower target lengths. However, in the case of IDN, much of the important information was also embedded in dialogue and was missed in the same way at higher target lengths.

Sample	%relevant (manual)	%coverage (manual)	ROUGE1 F1
IDN(b)	0.67	0.45	0.48
IDN(w)	0.40	0.30	0.36
Novel(b)	0.77	0.76	0.67
Novel(w)	0.07	0.01	0.05
Cnn (b)	1.0	1.0	1.0
Cnn (w)	0.0	0.0	0.02

Table 4: Analysis of best and worst ROUGE1 scoring generated summaries by SRL model. '% relevant' shows percentage of sentences in generated summary that match the ground truth abstractive summary (manual judgement used if there is a good sentence match or not). '% coverage' shows percentage of sentences in ground truth abstractive summary that match sentences in the generated summary.

5.2 Quality of Summaries from Best Model

Automatic metrics to evaluate summarisation is known to have many limitations (Fabbri et al., 2021). To get a better understanding of the quality of the summaries a manual inspection of the best and worst summaries from the best performing model for a non narrative (CNN/DM), narrative non interactive (Novel), and interactive narrative (IDN) was performed. The best performing models used were BS at length 3 for CNN/DM, SRL at length 27 for Novel, and SRL at length 81 for IDN. For each of the sentences in the model generated extractive summary, if it could be matched to any part of the abstractive summary it was marked as relevant. The number of relevant extracts divided by the total number of extracts is denoted as %relevant in table 4. For each sentence in the abstractive reference summary, if any part of the sentence could be matched to any of the extracted sentences it was marked as covered. The number of covered sentences divided by total number of sentences in the reference summary is denoted as %coverage in table 4. The corresponding ROUGE1 F1 score is also shown in the table for comparison.

The ROUGE metrics seems to capture relevance and coverage of sentences to some extent. The difference between best and worst summaries is less pronounced in case of IDN. This is because of shared text between datapoints and smaller differences between datapoints as discussed in section 3.2. However, the manual inspection of summaries revealed issues that were not reflected in the ROUGE scores. A sentence in the reference summary was marked covered if any of the sentences

Reference sentence from human written summary:
the dream abruptly ends with a truck crashing through william 's car .

Extracts:

[ex] s0 : chloe hears a horn three times and approaches william in panic .
a truck crashes into the left side of the car , hitting william , and then everything goes black .

Figure 3: Example of good quality extract

Reference sentence from human written summary:
upon a brief dialogue , in which rachel reveals the man they had seen at the park was her dad , and that he was cheating on her mother with that woman .

Extracts:

[ex] chloe : the ones who were making out ? [ex]
so when i saw he got a text from an unknown number ... asking him to meet ...

Figure 4: Example of low quality extract

in the model summary could be seen to be related to it. However, in most cases these sentences in the extractive summary do not convey all of the information that the corresponding parts of the abstractive reference summary do, even though both sets of sentences can be seen to be related. Additionally, the inspection suggests that even though many relevant extracts get picked up, the quality of selected extracts varies in terms of readability. To demonstrate the range of the quality of the selected extracts, Fig 3 shows an example of a high quality snippet of model summary and fig 4 shows and example of a low quality one. In the first example the information contained in the human written sentence is captured by the retrieved extracts. In case of the second example however, while it can be inferred that they are related, the information contained in the abstractive summary is not fully conveyed by the extracts and has poor readability. This issue is especially obvious in IDN where, due to its screenplay like structure, information captured by a single sentence in the abstractive summary is spread across several extracts. In CNN/DM on the other hand, information is presented in a concise way and sentences are dense with information.

6 Discussion

The main contribution of this piece of work is the generated IDN-Sum dataset. This is the first dataset for IDN that shows different branches that are possible through an interactive story. IDN is different from other forms of narrative text due to the presence of choice points that affect how the story unfolds. This dataset captures many different paths through such narratives. It is hence unique compared to other summarisation datasets because the high amount of overlapping text between data points. The dataset was created as a resource that enables us to investigate summarisation approaches for interactive and game narratives. It may also be used to study how summarisation models respond to small changes in text and target summary.

Capturing important differences between different playthroughs is a significant aspect of IDN summarisation. IDN is essentially a collection of linked literary documents. Summarization of multiple linked literary documents has not been studied previously, although multi-document summarization and plot (literary) summarization have been addressed separately. Unlike domains like news where multi document summarization(Antognini and Faltings, 2019) has been studied, IDN documents have a narrative structure and elements (plot, protagonist, emotions, etc) which influence the relative importance of sentences. The nature of differences between documents is different from domains like academic papers where comparative summarization has been studied(He et al., 2016). The differences are not solely topical and the links and link texts influences what is different between groups of documents. Therefore, this would also be a useful resource to study new NLP problems like comparative plot summarisation.

The dataset has 1250 playthroughs per episode and 8 episodes overall, but the code and JSONs for the ReaderBot will also be made available on GitHub[9]. This can be used to generate more playthroughs of the game, although they will need to be modified to adapt to different games. There are many types of IDN, both in terms of types of text and narrative design. While it is a limitation of this dataset that only one type of IDN is included, it takes a step towards making resources available for exploration of some aspects of IDN summarisation.

We also report and analyse performance of some standard baseline approaches quantitatively and qualitatively. In spite of a smaller number of data points, much longer input documents and difference in domain from CNN/DM, SummaRunner seems to scale for these longer documents and work well across domains, when considering ROUGE scores. However, manual inspection reveals several drawbacks of the ROUGE metric in terms of accurately reflecting summary quality. This is in line with findings from similar experiments performed on SummScreen in (Chen et al., 2021) where new entity centric evaluation metrics are pro-

[9]https://github.com/AshwathyTR/IDN-Sum

posed. Finding a good evaluation metric to assess summary quality is a known challenge, even in case of the CNN/DM dataset(Fabbri et al., 2021). For this reason, evaluation strategies usually include a human evaluation step in addition to automated metrics like ROUGE. However, in the case of narrative datasets, due to the large source length and relatively large reference summaries, human evaluation is resource intensive when compared to datasets like CNN/DM and more subjective since it needs to account for subjective aspects like coverage of plot points. Attempts to decrease subjectivity include strategies like judging the ability of the evaluator to answer questions about major plot points from the summary (Lapata, 2021). However, interactive narrative summarisation needs to account for interactive elements in addition to plot elements and important differences between playthroughs. Future work will augment this dataset with a similar list of plot points and interactive elements like decision points that can be used for evaluation.

The human written summaries against which scores are calculated summarise the entire IDN and represent variations between playthroughs through sentences like : *"If Chloe goes along with Rachel, she will be suspended. If Chloe takes the blame for Rachel, she will be expelled."* This means that in a playthrough where Chloe chose to take blame, there will be keywords relating explusion and in other branches, those relating suspension, but neither branch will have both. Hence, even if the model works perfectly, it cannot get a perfect ROUGE score since some of the keywords in the abstractive summary will not be present in that playthrough. Paraphrasing also causes some keywords to not be present in the original text. While these are drawbacks of the automatic evaluation, these scores give insight into relative performance of models and can be put into context by considering the score of the oracle as the upper bound and Random-N as the lower bound. These issues are mitigated by also providing ROUGE F1 scores against the oracle extractive reference summaries in Appendix B.

The qualitative analysis of the Oracle summaries also reveals some characteristics of narrative datasets that makes it worse if only keyword overlap is considered. News articles are structured differently to narrative text and are more likely to have summary sentences in the original text that capture the important information. Important information in narrative datasets are spread across several sentences. Presence of short sentences and sentences in utterances being broken up to include narration-like sentences in between screenplay-like text produces extracts that have high keyword overlap but are not useful or coherent. While scene-level summaries might be too large, selecting multi-sentence extracts instead of single sentence extracts might alleviate this issue to some extent. Additionally, sentences with many character names or short sentences with character names get high ROUGE scores even if they do not contain any relevant information because the reference summary contains them. A version of ROUGE that gives lower weights to words that are common in the document like the weighted ROUGE from(Ladhak et al., 2020) might do better in this regard. This study indicates that several aspects of the summarisation approaches that are commonly used for CNN/DM need to be re-examined and potentially redesigned for narrative and interactive narrative datasets, including: 1) The size and nature of extracts 2) automatic methods for conversion of abstractive summary to extractive summary 3) evaluation metrics and methodology. Hopefully, this dataset can help aid future research in these directions.

7 Conclusion

In this paper, we present the first summarisation dataset for interactive narratives. This was done by collecting fan made transcripts and abstractive summaries from Fandom and generating simulated playthroughs by assuming different combinations of choices. Annotation for extractive summarisation were created automatically from the abstractive summaries through greedy selection of extracts that maximised the ROUGE score with the abstractive summary. Even though narrative datasets have less data and longer text, SummaRunner with document truncation set to 3000 appears to scale when considering ROUGE scores. However, a qualitative analysis of generated summaries revealed several short comings in the ROUGE metric and oracle summaries suggesting that even though ROUGE scores for narrative datasets are comparable to CNN/DM, the summaries are not on the same level qualitatively. We hope that this dataset can be used for future research into better annotation methods, evaluation strategies. and summarisation approaches for interactive digital narratives.

References

Sanchit Agarwal, Nikhil Kumar Singh, and Priyanka Meel. 2018. Single-document summarization using sentence embeddings and k-means clustering. In *2018 International Conference on Advances in Computing, Communication Control and Networking (ICACCCN)*, pages 162–165.

Diego Antognini and Boi Faltings. 2019. Learning to create sentence semantic relation graphs for multi-document summarization. In *Proceedings of the 2nd Workshop on New Frontiers in Summarization*, pages 32–41, Hong Kong, China. Association for Computational Linguistics.

Marta Aparício, Paulo Figueiredo, Francisco Raposo, David Martins de Matos, Ricardo Ribeiro, and Luís Marujo. 2016. Summarization of films and documentaries based on subtitles and scripts. *Pattern Recognition Letters*, 73:7–12.

Camille Barot, Michael Branon, Rogelio Cardona-Rivera, Markus Eger, Michelle Glatz, Nancy Green, James Mattice, Colin Potts, Justus Robertson, Makiko Shukonobe, Laura Tateosian, Brandon Thorne, and R. Young. 2021. Bardic: Generating multimedia narratives for game logs. *Proceedings of the AAAI Conference on Artificial Intelligence and Interactive Digital Entertainment*, 13(2):154–161.

Iz Beltagy, Matthew E Peters, and Arman Cohan. 2020. Longformer: The long-document transformer. *arXiv preprint arXiv:2004.05150*.

Atef Chaudhury, Makarand Tapaswi, Seung Wook Kim, and Sanja Fidler. 2019. The shmoop corpus: A dataset of stories with loosely aligned summaries. *arXiv preprint arXiv:1912.13082*.

Mingda Chen, Zewei Chu, Sam Wiseman, and Kevin Gimpel. 2021. Summscreen: A dataset for abstractive screenplay summarization. *arXiv preprint arXiv:2104.07091*.

Yun-Gyung Cheong, Arnav Jhala, Byung-Chull Bae, and Robert Michael Young. 2008. Automatically generating summary visualizations from game logs. In *AIIDE*, pages 167–172.

Yue Dong, Yikang Shen, Eric Crawford, Herke van Hoof, and Jackie Chi Kit Cheung. 2018. Bandit-Sum: Extractive summarization as a contextual bandit. In *Proceedings of the 2018 Conference on Empirical Methods in Natural Language Processing*, pages 3739–3748, Brussels, Belgium. Association for Computational Linguistics.

Wafaa S El-Kassas, Cherif R Salama, Ahmed A Rafea, and Hoda K Mohamed. 2021. Automatic text summarization: A comprehensive survey. *Expert Systems with Applications*, 165:113679.

Alexander R. Fabbri, Wojciech Kryściński, Bryan McCann, Caiming Xiong, Richard Socher, and Dragomir Radev. 2021. SummEval: Re-evaluating summarization evaluation. *Transactions of the Association for Computational Linguistics*, 9:391–409.

Philip John Gorinski and Mirella Lapata. 2015. Movie script summarization as graph-based scene extraction. In *Proceedings of the 2015 Conference of the North American Chapter of the Association for Computational Linguistics: Human Language Technologies*, pages 1066–1076, Denver, Colorado. Association for Computational Linguistics.

Lei He, Wei Li, and Hai Zhuge. 2016. Exploring differential topic models for comparative summarization of scientific papers. In *Proceedings of COLING 2016, the 26th International Conference on Computational Linguistics: Technical Papers*, pages 1028–1038, Osaka, Japan. The COLING 2016 Organizing Committee.

Karl Moritz Hermann, Tomas Kocisky, Edward Grefenstette, Lasse Espeholt, Will Kay, Mustafa Suleyman, and Phil Blunsom. 2015. Teaching machines to read and comprehend. *Advances in neural information processing systems*, 28.

Faisal Ladhak, Bryan Li, Yaser Al-Onaizan, and Kathleen McKeown. 2020. Exploring content selection in summarization of novel chapters. In *Proceedings of the 58th Annual Meeting of the Association for Computational Linguistics*, pages 5043–5054, Online. Association for Computational Linguistics.

Pinelopi Papalampidi Frank Keller Mirella Lapata. 2021. Movie summarization via sparse graph construction.

Yang Liu. 2019. Fine-tune bert for extractive summarization. *arXiv preprint arXiv:1903.10318*.

Chanakya Malireddy, Srivenkata NM Somisetty, and Manish Shrivastava. 2018. Gold corpus for telegraphic summarization. In *Proceedings of the First Workshop on Linguistic Resources for Natural Language Processing*, pages 71–77.

Rada Mihalcea and Paul Tarau. 2004. TextRank: Bringing order into text. In *Proceedings of the 2004 Conference on Empirical Methods in Natural Language Processing*, pages 404–411, Barcelona, Spain. Association for Computational Linguistics.

David Millard, Charlie West-Taylor, Yvonne Howard, and Heather Packer. 2018. The ideal readerbot:: Machine readers and narrative analytics. In *NHT?18, July 2018, Baltimore, USA*. ACM.

MF Mridha, Aklima Akter Lima, Kamruddin Nur, Sujoy Chandra Das, Mahmud Hasan, and Muhammad Mohsin Kabir. 2021. A survey of automatic text summarization: Progress, process and challenges. *IEEE Access*, 9:156043–156070.

Ramesh Nallapati, Feifei Zhai, and Bowen Zhou. 2017. Summarunner: A recurrent neural network based sequence model for extractive summarization of documents. In *Thirty-first AAAI conference on artificial intelligence*.

Ramesh Nallapati, Bowen Zhou, Caglar Gulcehre, Bing Xiang, et al. 2016. Abstractive text summarization using sequence-to-sequence rnns and beyond. *arXiv preprint arXiv:1602.06023*.

Lawrence Page, Sergey Brin, Rajeev Motwani, and Terry Winograd. 1999. The pagerank citation ranking: Bringing order to the web. Technical report, Stanford InfoLab.

Pinelopi Papalampidi, Frank Keller, Lea Frermann, and Mirella Lapata. 2020. Screenplay summarization using latent narrative structure. In *Proceedings of the 58th Annual Meeting of the Association for Computational Linguistics*, pages 1920–1933, Online. Association for Computational Linguistics.

Revanth Rameshkumar and Peter Bailey. 2020. Storytelling with dialogue: A Critical Role Dungeons and Dragons Dataset. In *Proceedings of the 58th Annual Meeting of the Association for Computational Linguistics*, pages 5121–5134, Online. Association for Computational Linguistics.

Anna Marie Rezk and Mads Haahr. 2020. The case for invisibility: understanding and improving agency in black mirror's bandersnatch and other interactive digital narrative works. In *International Conference on Interactive Digital Storytelling*, pages 178–189. Springer.

BJ Sandesh and Gowri Srinivasa. 2017. A framework for the automated generation of paradigm-adaptive summaries of games. *International Journal of Computer Applications in Technology*, 55(4):276–288.

Quang Dieu Tran, Dosam Hwang, O Lee, Jai E Jung, et al. 2017. Exploiting character networks for movie summarization. *Multimedia Tools and Applications*, 76(8):10357–10369.

Jiacheng Xu, Zhe Gan, Yu Cheng, and Jingjing Liu. 2020. Discourse-aware neural extractive text summarization. In *Proceedings of the 58th Annual Meeting of the Association for Computational Linguistics*, pages 5021–5031, Online. Association for Computational Linguistics.

Weiwei Zhang, Jackie Chi Kit Cheung, and Joel Oren. 2019a. Generating character descriptions for automatic summarization of fiction. In *Proceedings of the AAAI Conference on Artificial Intelligence*, volume 33, pages 7476–7483.

Xingxing Zhang, Furu Wei, and Ming Zhou. 2019b. HIBERT: Document level pre-training of hierarchical bidirectional transformers for document summarization. In *Proceedings of the 57th Annual Meeting of the Association for Computational Linguistics*, pages 5059–5069, Florence, Italy. Association for Computational Linguistics.

Ming Zhong, Pengfei Liu, Yiran Chen, Danqing Wang, Xipeng Qiu, and Xuanjing Huang. 2020. Extractive summarization as text matching. In *Proceedings of the 58th Annual Meeting of the Association for Computational Linguistics*, pages 6197–6208, Online. Association for Computational Linguistics.

Qingyu Zhou, Nan Yang, Furu Wei, Shaohan Huang, Ming Zhou, and Tiejun Zhao. 2018. Neural document summarization by jointly learning to score and select sentences. In *Proceedings of the 56th Annual Meeting of the Association for Computational Linguistics (Volume 1: Long Papers)*, pages 654–663, Melbourne, Australia. Association for Computational Linguistics.

A Appendix A

Examples of the data are shown in this appendix. Appendix A.1 shows some lines from the beginning of a sample source document to be summarised. The complete document is not shown here due to its large size, but can be downloaded from the github repository. The corresponding lines from the human authored abstractive summary and aligned extractive summary is shown in appendix A.2 and appendix A.3 respectively. The complete summaries can be seen in the github page.

A.1 Example lines from preprocessed source text

S0 : ' [EX] :SC: S0 : Principal Wells, Rachel Amber, Joyce Price enter the office. [EX] PRINCIPAL WELLS : Ms. Price. How good of you to join us. [EX] JOYCE : I'm so sorry we're late. My—my shift ran late at the diner and then...just, sorry. [EX] PRINCIPAL WELLS : Let us proceed. One of you here is new to the Blackwell disciplinary process... And the other is all too familiar with it. Blackwell's code of conduct is built upon a foundation of mutual respect meant to foster an environment conducive to education and enrichment. When that respect is violated, actions are taken. When that respect is repeatedly disregarded, a more consequential response is required. [EX] CHLOE : (thinking) Okay, reality check time. Yesterday did actually happen. I ditched school with Rachel Amber. And then Rachel really did start that fire. And that was after we actually agreed to run away from here...right? [EX] PRINCIPAL WELLS : Are you paying attention to me, Chloe? [EX] CHLOE : Um...what? [EX] PRINCIPAL WELLS : Ms. Price, the last time we met, an agreement was brokered. Do you recall what that was? [EX] S0 : CHOICE: Don't screw up? [EX] CHLOE : Uh, don't get in trouble again? [EX] PRINCIPAL WELLS : Trouble is merely the byproduct, Ms. Price. What's at issue is your attitude. [EX] PRINCIPAL WELLS : We agreed that you would rededicate yourself to becoming an exemplary Blackwell citizen. [EX] CHLOE : We did? [EX] PRINCIPAL WELLS : In the event that you were unable or unwilling to do so, we also agreed that it would become pertinent to reassess your future status at the academy. Despite all this, you engaged in the following actions yesterday: Insubordinate language... [EX] S0 : CHOICE: (Trespassed on stage) [EX] PRINCIPAL WELLS : Disregarding posted signs about trespassing on the stage. [EX] PRINCIPAL WELLS : Shall I continue? [EX] S0 : CHOICE: (Didn't sabotage Victoria's homework) [EX] PRINCIPAL WELLS : Witnesses saying you were involved in bullying Nathan Prescott. [EX] S0 : CHOICE: (Didn't help Nathan) [EX] CHLOE : If "involved" means not sticking out my neck for Blackwell's richest asschild. I didn't realize that was a crime. [EX] PRINCIPAL WELLS : Your lack of awareness does not absolve you of anything, Ms. Price. [EX] S0 : CHOICE: (Was nice to Joyce) [EX] JOYCE : Say what you will about my daughter, but she is not a bully. [EX]

A.2 Example of human authored abstractive summary

Episode 2: Brave New World begins with Rachel Amber and Chloe Price in Principal Wells' office. Both Rachel and Chloe are questioned about their absence the day before. The conversation varies depending on how Chloe treated Joyce, if she sabotaged Victoria's homework, if she went onstage and smoked weed, whether she helped Nathan or not, and if she won or lost the backtalk against Drew (if she helped Nathan).

A.3 Example lines from automatically aligned extractive summary

I ditched school with Rachel Amber . [EX] S0 : CHOICE : (Did n't sabotage Victoria 's homework) [EX] PRINCIPAL WELLS : [EX] S0 : CHOICE : (Was nice to Joyce) [EX] PRINCIPAL WELLS : Mr. North 's situation requires ... sensitivity .

B ROUGE1 Scores against automatically aligned extractive summaries

Table 5 shows ROUGE1 scores computed against automatically aligned extractive summaries.

C ROUGE2 F1 Scores against human authored abstractive summaries

Table 6 shows ROUGE2 scores computed against human authored abstarctive summaries.

Dataset+Target Length	RN	LN	TR	BS	SR	LF	SRL
CnnDm3	0.34	0.5	0.45	0.51	**0.59**	N/A	N/A
Novel3	0.24	0.28	0.36	0.27	**0.38**	0.26	**0.38**
Novel9	0.38	0.38	0.42	0.38	0.42	0.41	**0.43**
Novel27	0.42	0.4	0.38	0.42	0.44	0.42	**0.47**
CRD3_3	0.11	0.14	0.23	0.1	0.11	0.19	**0.68**
CRD3_9	0.17	0.21	0.33	0.16	0.18	0.16	**0.74**
CRD3_27	0.31	0.31	0.42	0.26	0.32	0.45	**0.65**
CRD3_81	0.45	0.43	0.47	0.24	0.4	0.49	**0.61**
SB3	0.17	0.14	0.27	0.15	0.23	0.19	**0.36**
SB9	0.26	0.25	0.35	0.22	0.31	0.31	**0.44**
SB27	0.39	0.35	0.4	0.33	0.39	0.4	**0.49**
IDN3	0.15	0.23	0.21	0.07	0.34	0.22	**0.37**
IDN9	0.26	0.34	0.3	0.25	0.36	0.29	**0.45**
IDN27	0.39	0.41	0.4	0.34	0.44	0.4	**0.50**
IDN81	0.54	0.49	0.55	0.3	0.45	0.48	**0.62**

Table 5: ROUGE1 F1 scores against automatically aligned extractive summary

Dataset+Target Length	RN	LN	TR	BS	SR	LF	SRL
CnnDm3	0.084	0.174	0.143	0.177	**0.154**	N/A	N/A
Novel3	0.018	0.032	0.039	0.025	0.041	0.025	**0.042**
Novel9	0.039	0.05	**0.059**	0.046	0.056	0.053	**0.059**
Novel27	0.06	0.062	0.067	0.06	0.067	0.058	**0.074**
CRD3_3	0.005	0.005	0.018	0.004	0.004	0.007	**0.142**
CRD3_9	0.012	0.016	0.037	0.01	0.013	0.012	**0.244**
CRD3_27	0.031	0.03	0.067	0.024	0.038	0.119	**0.265**
CRD3_81	0.065	0.074	0.087	0.026	0.055	0.135	**0.255**
SB3	0.005	0.006	0.017	0.005	0.012	0.008	**0.021**
SB9	0.013	0.016	0.034	0.013	0.024	0.021	**0.041**
SB27	0.028	0.03	0.051	0.027	0.038	0.034	**0.061**
IDN3	0.004	0.011	0.009	0.002	0.011	0.009	**0.016**
IDN9	0.11	0.025	0.023	0.011	0.026	0.019	**0.03**
IDN27	0.03	0.038	0.05	0.03	0.047	0.04	**0.059**
IDN81	0.06	0.06	0.087	0.036	0.052	0.067	**0.096**

Table 6: ROUGE2 F1 scores against human authored abstractive summary

Summarization of Long Input Texts Using Multi-Layer Neural Network

Niladri Chatterjee, Aadyant Khatri and **Raksha Agarwal**
Indian Institute of Technology Delhi
Hauz Khas, Delhi-110016, India
{niladri@maths.iitd.ac.in, tt1191@iitd.ac.in, maz178296@maths.iitd.ac.in}

Abstract

The present paper describes the architecture of a novel Multi-Layer Long Text Summarizer (MLLTS) system proposed for the task of creative writing summarization. Typically, such writings are very long, often spanning over 100 pages. Summarizers available online are either not equipped enough to handle long texts, or even if they are able to generate the summary, the quality is poor. The proposed MLLTS system handles the difficulty by splitting the text into several parts. Each part is then subjected to different existing summarizers. A multi-layer network is constructed by establishing linkages between the different parts. During training phases, several hyper-parameters are fine-tuned. The system achieved very good ROUGE scores on the test data supplied for the contest.

1 Introduction

Summarization of long texts is a challenging problem for different widely available summarizers. While the Deep Learning (DL) based summarizer BART (Lewis et al., 2019) is severely restricted by the size of the input document, the quality of other traditional summarizers, namely LexRank (Erkan and Radev, 2004), TextRank (Mihalcea and Tarau, 2004) are found to be poor in terms of different ROUGE scores. The present paper proposes a novel architecture, Muti-Layer Long Text Summarizer (MLLTS), to overcome the above challenge. Figure 1 provides a schematic diagram of the proposed architecture.

The novelty of the MLLTS architecture is that it uses multiple online summarizers for carrying out the summarization task in the following way. First, the long input text is partitioned into several parts. These parts are assigned to different layers of the multi-layer architecture. If the document is partitioned into p parts and s is the number of summarizers used, then the total number of layers is $p \times s$. Different parameters are trained to fine-tune the intra-layer and inter-layer connections to optimize the overall output. Finally, VoteSumm method proposed by Agarwal and Chatterjee (2022) is used for generation of the summary, by combining different part summaries in an optimized manner.

The rest of the paper is organized as follows. Section 2 provides a brief review of some past works on network-based summarization. Section 3 presents a detailed description of the proposed architecture. Sections 4 and 5 describe the experiments conducted and the results obtained, respectively.

2 Related Past Works

Graph-based sentence ranking is a popular text summarization technique. In this approach, the input text is represented using a graph/network of sentence nodes. Edges between the nodes are created to represent the relationship between them. The nodes are ranked using different methods to determine their overall importance with respect to the given input text. Finally, the summary is generated by selecting the sentences which receive high ranks.

Mihalcea and Tarau (2004) used lexical similarity between sentences for edge creation in the graph and used PageRank (Brin and Page, 1998) to rank the nodes. Erkan and Radev (2011) used cosine similarity between bag-of-words representation of sentences for adding edges in the graph.

Tohalino and Amancio (2017) performed a summarization of multiple similar documents using multilayer networks. The layers of the network are used to represent each individual input document. TF-IDF based cosine similarity is used for connecting sentence nodes. Node ranking is performed via nine different network measurements, such as degree, strength, PageRank, accessibility, and symmetry, among others, for generation of summaries.

Alzuhair and Al-Dhelaan (2019) used a combination of different edge weighting schemes, namely

Proceedings of the 58th Annual Meeting of the Association for Computational Linguistics, pages 13–18
July 5–10, 2020. ©2020 Association for Computational Linguistics
https://doi.org/10.26615/978-954-452-056-4_002

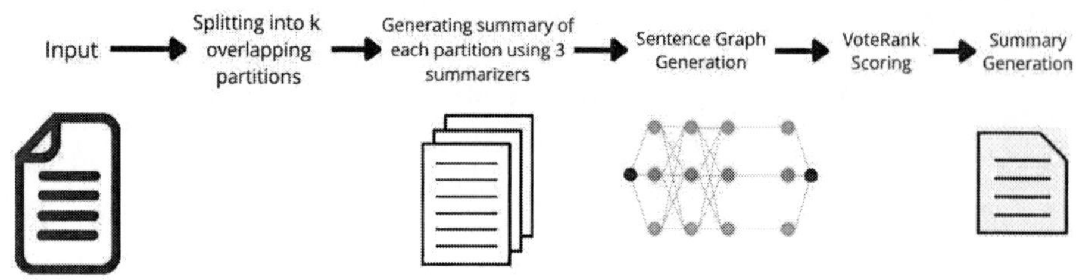

Figure 1

Jaccard similarity, TF-TDF similarity, Topic signature similarity and Identity similarity along with PageRank and HITS (Kleinberg, 1999) node ranking methods for summarization.

3 Proposed Approach: Multi-Layer Long Text Summarizer

The proposed MLLTS approach works in the following way. First, the long input text is partitioned into p smaller parts. These parts are not discrete, rather there is a 25% overlap between two successive parts. Then, each part is summarized using different summarizers. We have used three summarizers for the present work: TextRank, LexRank and Distil-BART.

The $3 \times p$ short texts thus formed, from the three summaries for each of the p parts for a long input text, constitute the different layers of a network graph. The sentences from these $3 \times p$ short texts form the nodes of the network graph and weighted edges are added between the nodes based on Jaccard similarity of the corresponding sentence vectors. Three parameters are fine-tuned to optimize the outputs. These are:

- K: used as a threshold to select a subset of edges of the network.
- α: that optimizes the strength of connections between sentences belonging to different parts.
- β: that finetunes the connection between sentences coming through the same summarizer.

For α and β, a value > 1 implies they strengthen the connections. Similarly, values < 1 weaken the strength. Once the network is prepared, VoteSumm technique is used to rank the nodes. The highest-ranking nodes are then used to generate the final summary.

However, one major challenge still faced is that the size of some partitions is still too long for DistilBART to generate a summary. Hence, we introduce the following novelty while partitioning the long input text. In such cases, the long input text is not partitioned into the p fixed number of parts. Rather, the partitioning is such that all the parts have a fixed number of words. The number of words is chosen such that DistilBART can generate a summary on it.

In our experiments, we discovered that the summaries generated by a fixed number of partitions exhibit better ROUGE scores. Hence, we kept this method to be the default option for partitioning. Partitioning on a fixed number of words is used only in situations discussed above.

4 Experimental Details

4.1 Dataset

The training data provided for the BookSum component of the Automatic Summarization for Creative Writing contest, was split into two parts, train-split, and validation-split. The train-split part had a total of 6759 samples, whereas the validation-split had 984 samples. The samples in the training set spanned 148 different books and 4931 chapters, with an average of 5424.32 words and 169.23 sentences. The corresponding target gold summaries had 362.26 words and 23.32 sentences on an average. There were 17 unique books and 636 chapters in the validation-split. These samples had 5097.17 words and 214.83 sentences on an average. Their gold summaries had 157.58 words and 10.35 sentences. The various statistics can be seen in Table 1.

4.2 Experiment – 1

As the first experiment, several summarizers provided in the SUMY package [`https://`

	Train-Split Inputs	Train-Split Target Summaries	Validation - Split Inputs	Validation - Split Target Summaries
Avg. no. of words	5424.32	362.26	5097.17	157.58
Max. no. of words	17928	2442	11010	741
Min. no. of words	754	41	899	23
Median no. of words	4523	307	4873	126
Avg. no. of sentences	169.23	23.32	214.83	10.35
Max. no. of sentences	591	126	562	48
Min. no. of sentences	10	2	9	2
Median no. of sentences	148.5	19	187.5	10

Table 1

`github.com/miso-belica/sumy`], a module for automatic summarization of text documents, were used separately on the input texts to generate the summaries. More specifically, we used the following summarizers:

- TextRank Summarizer
- Sum Basic Summarizer
- LSA Summarizer
- LexRank Summarizer
- Random Summarizer

Based on the ROUGE scores obtained, TextRank and LexRank summarizers were selected and used in the subsequent experiments. Table 2 provides the results obtained through Experiment-1. The ROUGE scores tabulated are the average scores obtained by different parameter sets over several input samples.

Summarizer	ROUGE 1	ROUGE 2	ROUGE SU4
TextRank Summarizer	0.142	0.018	0.033
Sum Basic Summarizer	0.140	0.016	0.033
LSA Summarizer	0.132	0.015	0.029
LexRank Summarizer	0.125	0.014	0.027
Random Summarizer	0.111	0.011	0.025

Table 2

4.3 Experiment – 2

In the second experiment the input was split into p parts. Then the above summarizers were used on each of the parts. For future reference these summaries will be called sub-summaries. These sub-summaries were then combined to obtain the summary for the whole text. In particular, we have worked with the values of $p \in \{3, 5, 8, 10\}$

The scores obtained by the whole text summaries thus generated from each of the summarizers were compared. It was hypothesized that using this method, important information from various parts of the input will be considered while generating the final summary. Results obtained through Experiment - 2 are given in Table 3.

Summarizer	ROUGE 1	ROUGE 2	ROUGE SU4
LexRank Summarizer	0.126	0.008	0.027
TextRank Summarizer	0.121	0.008	0.025

Table 3

4.4 Experiment – 3

As a variation to Experiment - 2, instead of directly appending the sub-summaries, the sub-summaries were fed into the VoteSumm technique to produce the final summary for the input. Apart from the number of partitions p, VoteSumm has two more hyper-parameters, K and α (as defined in Section 3).

We experimented with different sets of values for these parameters as given below:

$K \in \{0.1, 0.25, 0.5, 0.8\}$
$\alpha \in \{0.25, 0.3, 0.75, 1, 1.25, 1.5, 1.75, 2.0\}$

Along with TextRank and LexRank summarizers, state-of-the-art transformer-based summarizer (DistilBART) was also used. Table 4 contains the best five performing parameter sets in Experiment - 3.

α	p	K	ROUGE 1	ROUGE 2	ROUGE SU4
1.0	3	0.1	0.230	0.028	0.053
0.5	3	0.1	0.223	0.020	0.049
0.1	3	0.1	0.216	0.023	0.047
1.5	3	0.1	0.208	0.020	0.046
1.5	3	0.8	0.193	0.023	0.044

Table 4

4.5 Experiment – 4

In this experiment, different summarizers were no longer treated separately. Once the input was split into p parts, and the summaries for each of the parts were generated using the three summarizers (namely, LexRank, TextRank and DistilBART), all the $3 \times p$ sub-summaries were treated as different layers of VoteSumm to generate the combined summary. As before, p, K and α were varied, and the scores produced were compared. Along with these, a new hyper-parameter β was introduced (as defined in Section 3).

With the introduction of parameter β in conjunction with α, we experimented with two different combinations of them, namely ($\alpha + \beta$, $\alpha \times \beta$) to use them in VoteSumm. The following values of β were experimented with:

$$\beta \in \{0.25, 0.5, 0.75, 1, 1.25, 1.5, 1.75, 2.0\}$$

Our experiment here was to measure the efficacy of these two schemes in generating the whole-text summaries. Table 5 shows the five best performing parameter sets based on Experiment - 4.

α	β	p	K	Formula	ROUGE 1	ROUGE 2	ROUGE SU4
0.25	1.5	8	0.1	multiply	0.159	0.013	0.034
0.25	1.75	8	0.1	multiply	0.158	0.014	0.034
0.25	2.0	8	0.1	multiply	0.157	0.013	0.033
0.25	1.25	8	0.1	multiply	0.151	0.012	0.032
0.25	1.0	8	0.1	multiply	0.149	0.012	0.031

Table 5

4.6 Experiment – 5

In all the above experiments, the input was split into several discrete partitions. In this experiment, the input was split into p overlapping partitions. The rest was kept the same as in Experiment - 4. As a result of overlapping portions, a new hyper-parameter, 'partition-percent', came into consideration. The role of this hyper-parameter was to decide the percentage of overlap to be present in the partitions. In particular, we tried with values of 15% and 25%. The results of Experiment - 5 are given in Table 6.

α	β	p	K	Partition Percent	Formula	ROUGE 1	ROUGE 2	ROUGE SU4
0.3	2.5	8	0.1	25%	multiply	0.108	0.007	0.023
0.3	1.5	8	0.1	25%	multiply	0.108	0.007	0.023
0.3	2.0	8	0.1	25%	multiply	0.106	0.006	0.023
0.3	2.0	8	0.1	25%	add	0.105	0.006	0.023
0.3	2.5	8	0.1	25%	add	0.104	0.006	0.023

Table 6

4.7 Experiment – 6

While conducting Experiment – 5, we noticed that a significant number of sub-summaries could not be computed by DistilBART because of its limited input size. To overcome this, we introduced the following novelty in the proposed MLLTS architecture.

Instead of having a fixed number of splits for each of the input samples, the size of the split was fixed. This implied that the number of partitions may be different for different input texts as their sizes vary significantly. Hence in this experiment, the sizes of the partitions remained the same for all the input samples. Overlapping was also present in these partitions. Further, the three summarizers were used to generate summaries of p (not decided beforehand) parts of an input and then these $3 \times p$

sub-summaries were fed to VoteSumm. As before we experimented with different choices of the hyper - parameter values. The results of Experiment - 6 are in Table 7. Section 5 analyzes the results of different sets of experiments.

α	β	K	Partition Percent	Formula	ROUGE 1	ROUGE 2	ROUGE SU4
0.3	2.5	0.1	25%	multiply	0.116	0.008	0.026
0.3	1.5	0.1	25%	multiply	0.115	0.008	0.025
0.3	2.0	0.1	25%	multiply	0.115	0.008	0.025
0.3	2.5	0.1	25%	add	0.112	0.007	0.024
1.2	2.5	0.1	25%	multiply	0.112	0.006	0.024

Table 7

5 Results and Discussions

The results in the form of ROUGE scores obtained from Experiment - 1 and Experiment - 2 were not up to the mark. This was not surprising, and was rather intuitive since summarizers were directly applied to the input. However, there was a significant increase in the ROUGE scores from Experiment - 3 onwards. As given in Table - 4 the best five performing sets of parameters α, K and p are shown.

From the results of Experiment - 4, it became evident that having $p = 8$ and $K = 0.1$ yielded better results. Multiplying α and β to combine them and using higher values of β along with it also led to higher scores.

Once overlap was introduced between different partitions, combining α and β through addition also led to good scores. However, it was noted that having just 15% overlap did not improve the results but an overlap of 25% improved the results significantly. The best values for K and p again came out to be 0.1 and 8, respectively.

In Experiment – 6, where, p, the number of splits, was not pre-decided, the best results were obtained when α and β were multiplied to combine them, high values of β were used and K was set to be 0.1.

6 Conclusion

This paper proposes Multi-Layer Long Text Summarizer (MLLTS) as a possible solution of one of the modern day information processing problems, namely, summarization of long texts. Although a large number of summarizers have been developed and made available over the last decade, their performance on long text is highly questionable. The novel MLLTS system proposed in this work is our contribution towards this need. This is specially designed for the BookSum component of the Automatic Summarization for Creative Writing contest, COLING 2022. The input texts for this system were chapters from famous English books. The corresponding target summaries were expected to be of the order of 5% of the input text size.

A series of experiments were carried out to fine-tune several hyperparameters that are associated with the architecture. The successive design decisions and experiments are so planned that steady improvements in performance, with respect to ROUGE scores, can be observed. The best model, as per performance on the validation set, obtained values of 0.159 and 0.014 for ROUGE-1 and ROUGE - 2, respectively. However, on the test data, it achieved much better scores. For the test data, the ROUGE-1 and ROUGE-2 scores obtained were 0.2643 and 0.0471, respectively. Further, it obtained a ROUGE-L score of 0.2436. Test results also suggest pretty high scores with respect to several other metrics such as BERTScore and Litepyramid among others.

Encouraged by the results, we aim at working towards further improvements to the proposed MLLTS scheme.

References

Raksha Agarwal and Niladri Chatterjee. 2022. Votesumm: A multi-document summarization scheme using influential nodes of multilayer weighted sentence network.

Abeer Alzuhair and Mohammed Al-Dhelaan. 2019. An approach for combining multiple weighting schemes and ranking methods in graph-based multi-document summarization. *IEEE Access*, 7:120375–120386.

Sergey Brin and Lawrence Page. 1998. The anatomy of a large-scale hypertextual web search engine. *Computer Networks and ISDN Systems*, 30(1):107–117. Proceedings of the Seventh International World Wide Web Conference.

Günes Erkan and Dragomir R. Radev. 2011. Lexrank: Graph-based lexical centrality as salience in text summarization. *CoRR*, abs/1109.2128.

Jon M. Kleinberg. 1999. Authoritative sources in a hyperlinked environment. *J. ACM*, 46(5):604–632.

Mike Lewis, Yinhan Liu, Naman Goyal, Marjan Ghazvininejad, Abdelrahman Mohamed, Omer Levy, Veselin Stoyanov, and Luke Zettlemoyer. 2019. BART: denoising sequence-to-sequence pre-training for natural language generation, translation, and comprehension. *CoRR*, abs/1910.13461.

Rada Mihalcea and Paul Tarau. 2004. TextRank: Bringing order into text. In *Proceedings of the 2004 Conference on Empirical Methods in Natural Language Processing*, pages 404–411, Barcelona, Spain. Association for Computational Linguistics.

Jorge Valverde Tohalino and Diego R. Amancio. 2017. Extractive multi-document summarization using multilayer networks. *CoRR*, abs/1711.02608.

COLING 2022 Shared Task: LED Finteuning and Recursive Summary Generation for Automatic Summarization of Chapters from Novels

Prerna Kashyap
AWS New Apps Initiatives
Amazon, Seattle, USA
kaprerna@amazon.com

Abstract

We present the results of the Workshop on Automatic Summarization for Creative Writing 2022 Shared Task[1] on summarization of chapters from novels. In this task, we finetune a pretrained transformer model for long documents called LongformerEncoderDecoder which supports seq2seq tasks for long inputs which can be up to 16k tokens in length. We use the Booksum dataset for longform narrative summarization for training and validation, which maps chapters from novels, plays and stories to highly abstractive human written summaries. We use a summary of summaries approach to generate the final summaries for the blind test set, in which we recursively divide the text into paragraphs, summarize them, concatenate all resultant summaries and repeat this process until either a specified summary length is reached or there is no significant change in summary length in consecutive iterations. Our best model achieves a ROUGE-1 F-1 score of 29.75, a ROUGE-2 F-1 score of 7.89 and a BERT F-1 score of 54.10 on the shared task blind test dataset.

1 Introduction

Condensing long novel chapters into succinct and easy to digest summaries could be helpful as an informative bookmark to serve as a reminder of what happened in the last read chapter. This is much harder than other summarization tasks like summarizing news articles (Nallapati et al., 2016; Grusky et al., 2018; Narayan et al., 2018) or legal (Sharma et al., 2019) and scientific documents (Cohan et al., 2018). The reason for this is two fold. Firstly, the importance of automatic summarization systems for these tasks is diminished by the presence of article headlines, highlights or abstracts, as well as the length of the text to be summarized which is limited to a few hundred words to a few pages. Secondly, due to shorter text length and fact heavy content, there is no scope for extensive paraphrasing in the summaries. This is also due to short ranged causal and temporal dependencies and absence of convoluted plot lines. On the other hand, the task of summarizing chapters from novels (Ladhak et al., 2020; Kryściński et al., 2021) introduces all these additional challenges, including processing of long texts, abrupt changes in plot lines, dialogue and narration, and generation of highly abstractive summaries.

We present a recursive summary of summaries approach inspired by (Wu et al., 2021), where we decompose the long novel chapters into paragraphs and summarize them separately, thereby reducing computational complexity and noise in the target summaries. This is also similar to the divide and conquer approach used in (Gidiotis and Tsoumakas, 2020). These partial summaries are then combined to obtain an intermediate summary. This intermediate summary is then treated as the long text to be summarized and this process is repeated until either a final summary of a specified length is obtained or there is no significant change in summary length between consecutive intermediate summaries. The model used to generate these summaries is a pretained LongformerEncoderDecoder model[2] (Beltagy et al., 2020) finetuned on paragraph alignments obtained from the novel chapters. The datasets used for finetuning are described in Section 2 and the models are presented in Section 3. We present our results and analysis in Section 4.

2 Dataset

Some key challenges in long form summarization are computational constraints and limits on input length of pretrained models used for finetuning. To address these challenges, instead of using entire chapter to summary mappings, we use paragraph level alignments obtained for the novel chapters.

[1]https://creativesumm.github.io/sharedtask

[2]https://github.com/allenai/longformer

Proceedings of the 58th Annual Meeting of the Association for Computational Linguistics, pages 19–23
July 5–10, 2020. ©2020 Association for Computational Linguistics
https://doi.org/10.26615/978-954-452-056-4_003

The paragraph level alignments are computed between paragraphs extracted from chapters and individual sentences of chapter-level summaries, by leveraging paragraph-sentence similarity scores using a SentenceTransformer (Reimers and Gurevych, 2019) and a stable matching algorithm as mentioned in the Booksum paper (Kryściński et al., 2021).

We use two datasets for finetuning, one containing just the paragraph alignments (we will refer to this as Dataset 1) and another containing paragraph alignments along with a subset of the chapter to summary data with maximum chapter length constrained to 500 words (we will refer to this as Dataset 2). The maximum chapter length of 500 words is chosen because the maximum encoder and decoder length for the models is set to 512 and this ensures that a very small percentage of the total number of examples exceeds the maximum token length of 512 after tokenization. Before training, all chapter and summary text is cleaned by stripping away hyperlinks, multiple consecutive whitespaces and non ASCII characters. The number of examples for training and validation splits for both datasets can be seen in Table 1. Some statistics for the train and validation splits of both datasets after tokenization using the LED tokenizer can be found in Table 2 and Table 3 respectively. All lengths presented in the table are number of words in the text.

3 Models

The reference summaries for the novel chapters are highly abstractive with high semantic and low lexical overlap. The novel chapters have long range causal and temporal dependencies that can be effectively captured by the self attention component in transformers (Vaswani et al., 2017), which enables the network to capture contextual information. However, the memory and computational requirements of self-attention grow quadratically with sequence length, making it very expensive for longer texts like novel chapters. Longformer (Beltagy et al., 2020) is a modified transformer with a self-attention operation that scales linearly with the sequence length, making it a lucrative option for processing long sequences.

We use the led-base-16384[3] LongformerEncoderDecoder model for finetuning, which is initialized from bart-base[4] (Lewis et al., 2019) since both models share the exact same architecture. We finetune the pretrained LED base model on the two datasets mentioned in Section 2 for 10 epochs and evaluate on the validation split after every 3000 steps. Model outputs are decoded using beam search with 2 beams and n-gram repetition blocking for n > 3. The LED config min and max length is set to 100 and 512 respectively, with a length penalty of 2.0, early stopping set to False and a batch size of 1 due to computational constraints. The maximum encoder and decoder length is set to 512.

In addition to the usual attention mask, LED can make use of an additional global attention mask defining which input tokens are attended globally and which are attended only locally, just as in the case of Longformer. We follow recommendations of the paper (Beltagy et al., 2020) and use global attention only for the very first token and we ensure that no loss is computed on padded tokens by setting their index to -100. We also disable gradient checkpointing and the caching mechanism to save memory. We use the ROUGE metric (Lin, 2004) for evaluation during model training and validation.

4 Experiments and Results

We train two models on Dataset 1 and 2 (referred to as Model 1 and Model 2 respectively) and choose the model with the best overall validation score for final submission for the shared task. The mid ROUGE F-1 scores on the validation set of Dataset 1 and 2 for both models can be found in Table 4.

For the final submission for the shared task, the final summaries for input novel chapters are generated using the recursive summary of summaries method described in the previous sections. The novel chapters in the blind test dataset are divided into paragraphs not exceeding 400 words in length, with an overlap of one sentence per chunk. This means that the last sentence from the previous paragraph chunk becomes the first sentence of the new paragraph chunk. If addition of any sentence to a chunk exceeds the chunk size of 400 words, that sentence becomes a part of the next chunk. These chunks are then summarized separately and concatenated in a recursive fashion to get the final summary. We observe that the training data has a mean summary to chapter length ratio of 0.15 and a standard deviation of 0.20 (where length is considered

[3]https://huggingface.co/allenai/led-base-16384

[4]https://huggingface.co/facebook/bart-base

Dataset	Train split	Val split	# of unique train books	# of unique val books
Dataset 1	13720	2334	53	11
Dataset 2	14208	2486	82	15

Table 1: Training and validation splits for datasets used.

Dataset	Mean-article-len	Mean-summary-len	%-article-len > 512	%-summary-len > 512
Dataset 1	204.77	40.00	0.03	0.00
Dataset 2	213.04	45.31	0.04	0.00

Table 2: Train split stats after tokenization for datasets used.

Dataset	Mean-article-len	Mean-summary-len	%-article-len > 512	%-summary-len > 512
Dataset 1	189.99	38.88	0.02	0.00
Dataset 2	205.65	43.53	0.04	0.00

Table 3: Validation split stats after tokenization for datasets used.

to be number of words in the text). So, during the generation of summaries by the finetuned model, we keep the maximum predicted summary length to be 35% of the input chapter length i.e. mean plus standard deviation of the summary to chapter length ratio of training datasets. This means that the input text is decomposed into paragraphs and intermediate summaries are created by generating individual summaries of these paragraphs and concatenating them until summary length of atmost 35% of the input text is reached or consecutive intermediate summary lengths are within 200 words of each other. The final evaluation metrics of the best performing model i.e. Model 1 on the shared task's blind test set can be found in Table 5.

4.1 Qualitative Analysis

A brief qualitative analysis of the predicted summaries in comparison to the reference summaries yields a few important observations. Examples of reference and predicted summaries from the Booksum validation dataset using Model 1 and recursive summary generation can be seen in Table 6. The highlighted portions of both summaries indicate the semantically relevant parts and it is evident that the predicted summary manages to capture most of important information from the chapter accurately. The text presented in red color in the predicted summary section indicates grammatically or factually inaccurate sentences in the summary, which accounts for a small percentage of the overall predicted summary. One problem that the model generated summaries frequently suffer from is repetition (which often results in nonsensical sentences) as seen in Example 3 in Table 6. The model generated summaries also lack coherence due to generation of summaries of independent paragraphs.

4.2 Model Limitations and Future Work

Due to computational constraints, the full power of the LED model, in which input length up to 16k tokens can be used, could not be leveraged and the encoder decoder maximum length was limited to 512 tokens. Also, the abstractive nature of the reference summaries makes lexical overlap measured by ROUGE (Lin, 2004) an inadequate metric for model evaluation and can be substituted with BERTScore (Zhang* et al., 2020) or SummaQA (Scialom et al., 2019) which leverage pretrained neural models.

Deciding the maximum length of the final summary for input text during the recursive summary generation method is also a problem, because the current value of 35% of input text length might throw away important information or incorporate information that isn't too relevant. Other methods apart from plain concatenation to generate a final summary using intermediate summaries can also be considered a part of future work.

Acknowledgements

We would like to thank our colleagues Stephen Vilke, Mark Andress, Bobby Williams and Monica Hu, who helped in reviewing and assisting in the writing of this paper and facilitating more research opportunities within the team.

Model	Dataset	ROUGE-1	ROUGE-2	ROUGE-L	ROUGE-LSUM
Model 1	Dataset 1	19.13	4.83	13.51	13.52
Model 2	Dataset 1	18.41	4.60	13.20	13.20
Model 1	Dataset 2	19.46	4.85	13.60	13.97
Model 2	Dataset 2	18.69	4.58	13.25	13.25

Table 4: Validation scores for finetuned models on validation splits of all datasets used.

ROUGE-1	ROUGE-2	ROUGE-L	BERTScore-F1	SummaCZS	LitePyramid-l3c
29.75	7.89	28.33	54.10	15.62	6.91

Table 5: Final evaluation metrics for Model 1 on shared task blind test set.

References

Iz Beltagy, Matthew E. Peters, and Arman Cohan. 2020. Longformer: The long-document transformer. *arXiv:2004.05150*.

Arman Cohan, Franck Dernoncourt, Doo Soon Kim, Trung Bui, Seokhwan Kim, Walter Chang, and Nazli Goharian. 2018. A discourse-aware attention model for abstractive summarization of long documents. In *Proceedings of the 2018 Conference of the North American Chapter of the Association for Computational Linguistics: Human Language Technologies, Volume 2 (Short Papers)*, pages 615–621, New Orleans, Louisiana. Association for Computational Linguistics.

Alexios Gidiotis and Grigorios Tsoumakas. 2020. A divide-and-conquer approach to the summarization of long documents. *IEEE/ACM Transactions on Audio, Speech, and Language Processing*, 28:3029–3040.

Max Grusky, Mor Naaman, and Yoav Artzi. 2018. Newsroom: A dataset of 1.3 million summaries with diverse extractive strategies. In *Proceedings of the 2018 Conference of the North American Chapter of the Association for Computational Linguistics: Human Language Technologies, Volume 1 (Long Papers)*, pages 708–719, New Orleans, Louisiana. Association for Computational Linguistics.

Wojciech Kryściński, Nazneen Rajani, Divyansh Agarwal, Caiming Xiong, and Dragomir Radev. 2021. Booksum: A collection of datasets for long-form narrative summarization.

Faisal Ladhak, Bryan Li, Yaser Al-Onaizan, and Kathleen R. McKeown. 2020. Exploring content selection in summarization of novel chapters. *CoRR*, abs/2005.01840.

Mike Lewis, Yinhan Liu, Naman Goyal, Marjan Ghazvininejad, Abdelrahman Mohamed, Omer Levy, Veselin Stoyanov, and Luke Zettlemoyer. 2019. Bart: Denoising sequence-to-sequence pre-training for natural language generation, translation, and comprehension. *arXiv preprint arXiv:1910.13461*.

Chin-Yew Lin. 2004. ROUGE: A package for automatic evaluation of summaries. In *Text Summarization Branches Out*, pages 74–81, Barcelona, Spain. Association for Computational Linguistics.

Ramesh Nallapati, Bowen Zhou, Cicero dos Santos, Çağlar Gulçehre, and Bing Xiang. 2016. Abstractive text summarization using sequence-to-sequence RNNs and beyond. In *Proceedings of The 20th SIGNLL Conference on Computational Natural Language Learning*, pages 280–290, Berlin, Germany. Association for Computational Linguistics.

Shashi Narayan, Shay B. Cohen, and Mirella Lapata. 2018. Don't give me the details, just the summary! topic-aware convolutional neural networks for extreme summarization. In *Proceedings of the 2018 Conference on Empirical Methods in Natural Language Processing*, pages 1797–1807, Brussels, Belgium. Association for Computational Linguistics.

Nils Reimers and Iryna Gurevych. 2019. Sentence-bert: Sentence embeddings using siamese bert-networks. In *Proceedings of the 2019 Conference on Empirical Methods in Natural Language Processing*. Association for Computational Linguistics.

Thomas Scialom, Sylvain Lamprier, Benjamin Piwowarski, and Jacopo Staiano. 2019. Answers unite! unsupervised metrics for reinforced summarization models. *CoRR*, abs/1909.01610.

Eva Sharma, Chen Li, and Lu Wang. 2019. Bigpatent: A large-scale dataset for abstractive and coherent summarization. *ArXiv*, abs/1906.03741.

Ashish Vaswani, Noam Shazeer, Niki Parmar, Jakob Uszkoreit, Llion Jones, Aidan N. Gomez, Lukasz Kaiser, and Illia Polosukhin. 2017. Attention is all you need.

Jeff Wu, Long Ouyang, Daniel M. Ziegler, Nissan Stiennon, Ryan Lowe, Jan Leike, and Paul Francis Christiano. 2021. Recursively summarizing books with human feedback. *ArXiv*, abs/2109.10862.

Tianyi Zhang*, Varsha Kishore*, Felix Wu*, Kilian Q. Weinberger, and Yoav Artzi. 2020. Bertscore: Evaluating text generation with bert. In *International Conference on Learning Representations*.

Chapter and Book	Reference summary	Predicted Summary
Antony and Cleopatra, Act 2, Scene 1	Messina. Pompey's house. Pompey discusses strategy with his men, Menas and Menecrates, confidently assessing his fortunes. When Menas reports that Lepidus and Octavius Caesar are in the field against him, Pompey dismisses it: they wait in Rome, helpless without Antony. Pompey is counting on Antony to stay in Egypt with Cleopatra. Varrius enters with bad news: Antony has returned. Pompey is distressed, as Antony is by far the best soldier of the triumvirate. Menas hopes that Antony and Octavius will not be able to work together, due to the fact that Antony's brother and late wife warred against Octavius, but Pompey points out that natural enemies may band together against a common threat.	Messina. Pompey's house. Menecrates and Menas discuss the fact that Antony and Cleopatra are in Egypt together. Menas tells Pompey that he cannot hope Caesar and Lepidus to meet in Rome together, as Antony is already in Rome. Menass tells him that he has a message for Antony, and he tells him he will deliver it in a day or two. He tells Menas that he will give Antony a room for further travel.
Much Ado About Nothing, Act 5, Scene 3	Claudio, Don Pedro and several other men visit Hero's gravesite and perform a short memorial service. Claudio has written an epitaph for Hero, after which he sings a song and then promises to perform the same ritual every year. Don Pedro bids the other men good night and takes Claudio with him to Leonato's house.	Claudio, Don Pedro, and the Musicians all go to Hero's tomb and sing a hymn to honor Hero's memory. Claudio and Don Pedro leave the tomb to bid farewell to Hero. The crowd sings a song to Hero, and then they all leave to go to Leonato to bid goodbye to the Hero. Don Pedro and Claudio leave to say a prayer to Hero to be buried in the morning. The rest of the group leaves to go and bid farewell Hero to Claudio.
Antony and Cleopatra, Act 4, Scene 4	The following day, Eros arms Antony for battle, and Cleopatra insists on helping. Antony feels confident about the coming fight, promising Cleopatra that anyone who attempts to undo his armor before he is ready to remove it and rest will confront his rage. An armed soldier enters and reports that a thousand others stand ready for Antony's command. Antony bids Cleopatra adieu, kisses her, and leads his men into battle.	Alexandria. Cleopatra's palace. Antony and Cleopatra arrive and Eros kisses her goodbye. The officer then kisses her and tells her to go to the port and come back. The soldier then leaves and the rest of the soldiers arrive. The soldiers then leave, and Antony kisses Cleopatra goodbye. He kisses her farewell and leaves. The officers then go off to battle, and he kisses her. The guards then leave and the soldiers go to battle.

Table 6: Examples of reference and predicted summaries from the Booksum validation dataset.

TEAM UFAL @ CreativeSumm 2022: BART and SamSum based few-shot approach for creative Summarization

Rishu Kumar and **Rudolf Rosa**
ÚFAL, Charles University
lastname@ufal.mff.cuni.cz

Abstract

This system description paper details TEAM UFAL's approach for the SummScreen, TVMegasite subtask of the CreativeSumm shared task. The subtask deals with creating summaries for dialogues from TV Soap operas. We utilized BART based pre-trained model fine-tuned on SamSum dialouge summarization dataset. Few examples from AutoMin dataset and the dataset provided by the organizers were also inserted into the data as a few-shot learning objective. The additional data was manually broken into chunks based on different boundaries in summary and the dialogue file. For inference we choose a similar strategy as the top-performing team at AutoMin 2021, where the data is split into chunks, either on [SCENE_CHANGE] or exceeding a pre-defined token length, to accommodate the maximum token possible in the pre-trained model for one example. We implemented two different strategies as splits on [SCENE_CHANGE] did not necessarily mean having less than 1024 tokens in a segment.

1 Introduction

Creative Summarization as a field is rather novel, which neatly exists between document summarization and Conversation Summarization. The task of summarization focuses on extracting relevant information from the entire document where the task of minuting includes an additional objective of getting rid of redundancies in the dialogues as well as extracting relevant information based on different boundaries within the text i.e. topic switching. It is written, proof-read and mostly contains of coherent and grammatically correct sentences, and since it is also supposed to mimic how people speak, it also contains grammatically incorrect sentences as well as people speaking over each other. Thus, this track of research has a unique opportunity to leverage the recent advances in document summarization and Automatic Minuting. Unlike the dataset used for Automated Minuting, the dataset in this subtask carries a special property where the conversation changes are marked with special tokens such as [SCENE_CHANGE] with on average a transcript containing 20±14, Scene breaks across training, test and dev dataset splits. Since the dataset consists of transcripts from different shows, which presumably are written by different screenplay writers resulting in different writing style, which explains the very high standard deviation on how often SCENE_CHANGE is there in a transcript. While this approach makes it easier to split a transcript into multiple parts, it does not guarantee that the segments will not exceed the tokens limits of the pre-trained model, 1024 in our case.

The task for summarizing a TV show episode introduces a unique challenge compared to the task of summarizing a conversation. The transcripts for TV shows not only contain the dialogues, it also contains visual cue descriptions which are absent from the Minuting Summarization task as shown in . However, on a broad sense these tasks share some similarities as a summary can constructed from the perspective of one character in the show can be polar opposite to the summary generated from the perspective of a different character. Previous approaches to the multi-party summarization includes modeling intra-speaker and inter-speaker topics with random walk in a graph (Chen and Metze, 2012), leveraged word-embeddings (Shang et al., 2018) by using WordNet (Miller, 1995) to make summary more abstractive. The word-embedding based approach was further incorporated by (Zhao et al., 2019), and (Li et al., 2019) with different model architecture with (Li et al., 2019) incorporating information from visual modality into their summarization model.

Our approach in this subtask builds upon the ideas introduced in these papers, in training and inferences. We incorporate a pipeline with three components, Model, Data Cleaning and Inference

Proceedings of the 58th Annual Meeting of the Association for Computational Linguistics, pages 24–28
July 5–10, 2020. ©2020 Association for Computational Linguistics
https://doi.org/10.26615/978-954-452-056-4_004

Figure 1: A snippet from the training dataset of SummScreen ForeverDreaming split

```
( ENTITY75 runs and climb@@ s up a sta@@ ir@@ well outside . Inside , a few doctors g
ather around Pat@@ el . )
DOCTOR : S@@ cal@@ p@@ el .
( Pat@@ el lays , unconscious . ENTITY75 breaks a cage outside and climb@@ s inside .
 At the operation , a doctor makes an inc@@ ision on Pat@@ el 's chest . Someone else
 wi@@ pes the blood away . ENTITY75 , climb@@ ing above where the operation is taking
 place , moves through an entr@@ y@@ way and gasps as her legs dang@@ le below throug
h a giant hole in the wal@@ k@@ way . She pulls herself up , grun@@ ting . On her han
ds and knees , she looks down . Coming up to another hole in the ceiling above where
the doctors are cur@@ r@@ ently cutting Pat@@ el open , she gets a better look with a
 small tele@@ scope that is about the size of a pen@@ cil . She see@@ es ENTITY69 bel
ow , ob@@ serving the operation . And ENTITY39 . She gets a better look . She sees Pa
t@@ el 's face . They 're making the inc@@ ision deeper . One of the doctors hol@@ d@
@ ds a small metal ca@@ sing that is for@@ med into a half moon . )
ENTITY69 : Uh , careful with that . That 's the equi@@ val@@ ent to three hundred pou
nds of T@@ N@@ T .
ENTITY39 : Yes . Do n't kill him .
( ENTITY75 watches in horror as the doctors put the bomb inside Pat@@ el 's chest . )
```

Table 1: A brief description of the SummScreen ForeverDreaming

		Transcript		Summaries	
Data Split	#Examples	Avg. word_count	Std. Dev	Avg. word_count	Std. Dev
train	18915	6360	±1612	380	±237
dev	1795	6336	±1591	380	±234
test	1793	6348	±1599	382	±247

as discussed in following sections.

2 Dataset

CreatievSumm shared task recommends using SummScreen (Chen et al., 2022) for training, evaluation and testing purposes. It is divided into two parts based on the source of collection, i.e. The TV MegaSite (TMS) and ForeverDreaming(FD). For our system, we chose to work with ForeverDreaming part of the SummScreen dataset. This split in turn is released into two forms, one is anonymized where character names are replaced by "ENTITY", and another is the normal transcript with character names present. For our submission, we chose to work with anonymized version of the dataset, which was in-line with AutoMin (Ghosal et al., 2021) dataset.

Figure 1 provides a glimpse of how data looked in its original phase. We first began by sanitizing the data and removing information which was not relevant to us. Our sanitization process included removing @@, and using MosesTokenizer (Koehn et al., 2007) to fix the tokenization in the dataset. We also implemented various regex expansion to convert *I'm* $\rightarrow$ *I am*, *..shouldn't* $\rightarrow$ *..should not*. After a qualitative overview of the dataset in all splits, we implemented more rule-based text processing such as removing the additional information which did not include a character's action. Among such rules, one was to remove the line if it did not start with "ENTITY" after cleaning all the punctuations and extra space. We also change dialogues such as "ENTITY1 Laughs" to "ENTITY1 : Laughs" to reduce the number of lines removed from the dataset for not being a conversational utterance.

We added 16 examples from the dataset with high number of [SCENE_BREAK] and sentence count in summaries. The mixture of dataset is visualized in Figure 3. We manually split the summaries based on the relevant splits of the transcript. We also implement similar measures for the AutoMin dataset, where we also sampled eight transcripts and their corresponding summaries. The relevant statistics for the SummScreen ForeverDreaming dataset is included in Table 1.

3 Result

Table 2 and 3 presents the official results on the test set as calculated by the organizers. Our submission performs on par with other teams and achieves a higher average number of words per summary while getting similar automated evaluation scores. It is also worth mentioning that since our model was trained on ananomized data from AutoMin

Figure 2: The training regime we used to introduce different conversational style from the training dataset and AutoMin dataset to the SamSum datset

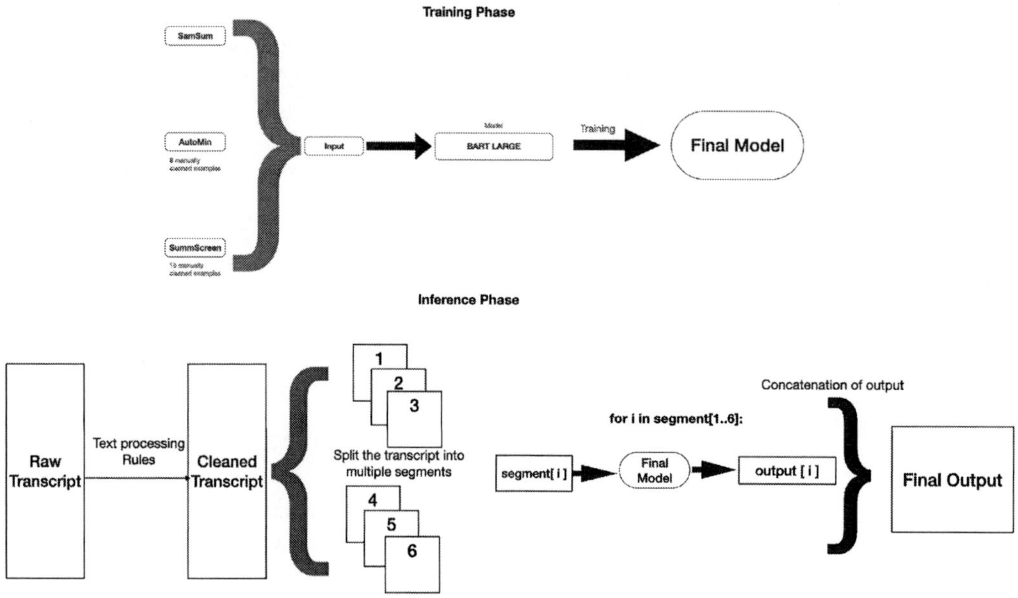

Table 2: Official Results – part I

	ROUGE-1	ROUGE-2	ROUGE-L	BERTScore-P	BERTScore-R	BERTScore-F1	LitePyramid-p2c
LED_1024	0.1428	0.0154	0.1236	0.4100	0.4107	0.4052	0.1371
LED_4096	0.1694	0.0209	0.1501	0.4591	0.4752	0.4600	0.0337
LED_16384	0.1514	0.0170	0.1334	0.4485	0.4632	0.4489	0.0337
inotum_summscreen-fd.jsonl	0.2860	0.0624	0.2529	0.5934	0.5609	0.5750	0.0673
team_ufal_fd.json	0.2469	0.0408	0.2300	0.5038	0.5590	0.5285	0.0472
AMRTVSumm_summscreen-fd.jsonl	0.2307	0.0303	0.2106	0.4906	0.5344	0.5108	0.0116

shared task and the training files for this shared task, our output suffers from cases where the name resolution has not been perfect.

4 Methodology

For our experiment, we use pre-trained BART (Lewis et al., 2019) from Facebook research, released as a pre_trained model on XSum (Narayan et al., 2018) on Hugging-Face (Wolf et al., 2019). We further fine-tuned the model on SamSum dataset. The exact implementation for our models is released publicly on GitHub[1]. We are also releasing the performance of different pre-trained models, such as T5 for zero-shot and few-shot learning on SummScreen ForeverDreaming dataset For inference, we use the same strategy as (Shinde et al., 2021)'s model for AutoMin2021. We split the transcript into multiple chunks of dialogues. This split is done either on [SCENE_BREAK] occurrence or when the token count exceeds a pre-defined limit. This helps us in extracting all the relevant information from the data without losing any information in truncation.

BART is a denoising autoencoder used to pre-trained seq-to-seq models for Natural Language Generation among other tasks. During the training of this model, a random denoising function is used to corrupt the text and then it learns how to recover the original text. It is also capable of operating bi-directionally on sequence generation unlike BERT (Devlin et al., 2018). We primarily focused on this training strategy because of its proven results on AutoMin shared task.

During inference as depicted in Figure 2, we split the conversation into chunks, and concatenate the output to construct final output.

5 Conclusion

In this system description paper, we explain the training regime we used to participate in the CreativeSumm shared task using SummScreen Forever-

[1]https://github.com/pyRis/creative_summ_subm

Figure 3: The training regime we used to introduce different conversational style from the training dataset and AutoMin dataset to the SamSum datset

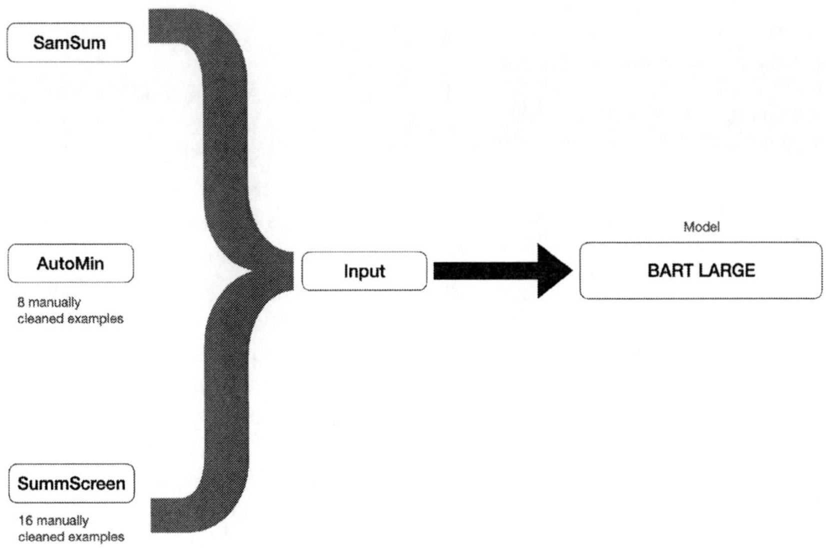

Table 3: Official results – part II

	LitePyramid-p2c	LitePyramid-l2c	LitePyramid-p3c	LitePyramid-l3c	SummaCZS	Length	Density	Coverage	Novel 1-grams	Novel 2-grams
LED_1024	0.1371	0.1200	0.0987	0.0878	0.0559	330	1.1440	0.7148	0.3060	0.7801
LED_4096	0.0337	0.0069	0.0304	0.0049	0.1052	188	1.4378	0.7343	0.2803	0.7314
LED_16384	0.0337	0.0069	0.0304	0.0049	0.1644	192	1.5474	0.7108	0.2904	0.7285
inotum_summscreen-fd.jsonl	0.0673	0.0560	0.0559	0.0534	0.0272	86	1.0321	0.6664	0.3715	0.8251
team_ufal_fd.json	0.0472	0.0229	0.0406	0.0191	0.1282	289	2.0821	0.7127	0.2484	0.6498
AMRTVSumm_summscreen-fd.jsonl	0.0116	0.0008	0.0138	0.0007	0.024	256	0.8789	0.6137	0.4924	0.8569

Dreaming dataset. Our system incorporates mixing of training samples from novel datasets into an existing dataset, which resembles a few-shot approach. In Section 6, we propose the direction we would like to take for incorporating the shared task training dataset into training.

6 Future Work

While we observe that zero-shot / few-shot learning creates coherent looking outputs, the problem to train on the complete data-set still remains open. Attributed to the lack of segment-wise summary data for longer transcripts, splitting text into segments for training does not work without loosing information or wrong alignment of text with corresponding line with summary. We plan to release our experiments on GitHub repository highlighting the issue, and the performance of the model on such training regime. This direction of research into a semi-supervised splitting of transcript and summary can help with the current problem of exceeding maximum length for tokenization.

Acknowledgements

Rishu Kumar has received financial support from the EMLCT programme[2] as part of his graduate study.

References

Mingda Chen, Zewei Chu, Sam Wiseman, and Kevin Gimpel. 2022. Summscreen: A dataset for abstractive screenplay summarization. In *ACL*.

Yun-Nung (Vivian) Chen and Florian Metze. 2012. Integrating intra-speaker topic modeling and temporal-based inter-speaker topic modeling in random walk for improved multi-party meeting summarization. In *INTERSPEECH*.

Jacob Devlin, Ming-Wei Chang, Kenton Lee, and Kristina Toutanova. 2018. Bert: Pre-training of deep bidirectional transformers for language understanding. *arXiv preprint arXiv:1810.04805*.

Tirthankar Ghosal, Ondřej Bojar, Muskaan Singh, and Anja Nedoluzhko. 2021. Overview of the First

[2]https://lct-master.org

Shared Task on Automatic Minuting (AutoMin) at Interspeech 2021. In *Proc. First Shared Task on Automatic Minuting at Interspeech 2021*, pages 1–25.

Philipp Koehn, Hieu T. Hoang, Alexandra Birch, Chris Callison-Burch, Marcello Federico, Nicola Bertoldi, Brooke Cowan, Wade Shen, Christine Moran, Richard Zens, Chris Dyer, Ondrej Bojar, Alexandra Constantin, and Evan Herbst. 2007. Moses: Open source toolkit for statistical machine translation. In *ACL*.

Mike Lewis, Yinhan Liu, Naman Goyal, Marjan Ghazvininejad, Abdelrahman Mohamed, Omer Levy, Ves Stoyanov, and Luke Zettlemoyer. 2019. Bart: Denoising sequence-to-sequence pre-training for natural language generation, translation, and comprehension.

Manling Li, Lingyu Zhang, Heng Ji, and Richard J. Radke. 2019. Keep meeting summaries on topic: Abstractive multi-modal meeting summarization. In *Proceedings of the 57th Annual Meeting of the Association for Computational Linguistics*, pages 2190–2196, Florence, Italy. Association for Computational Linguistics.

George A. Miller. 1995. Wordnet: A lexical database for english. *Commun. ACM*, 38(11):39–41.

Shashi Narayan, Shay B. Cohen, and Mirella Lapata. 2018. Don't give me the details, just the summary! Topic-aware convolutional neural networks for extreme summarization. In *Proceedings of the 2018 Conference on Empirical Methods in Natural Language Processing*, Brussels, Belgium.

Guokan Shang, Wensi Ding, Zekun Zhang, Antoine Tixier, Polykarpos Meladianos, Michalis Vazirgiannis, and Jean-Pierre Lorré. 2018. Unsupervised abstractive meeting summarization with multi-sentence compression and budgeted submodular maximization. In *Proceedings of the 56th Annual Meeting of the Association for Computational Linguistics (Volume 1: Long Papers)*, pages 664–674, Melbourne, Australia. Association for Computational Linguistics.

Kartik Shinde, Nidhir Bhavsar, Aakash Bhatnagar, and Tirthankar Ghosal. 2021. Team abc@ automin 2021: Generating readable minutes with a bart-based automatic minuting approach. *Proceedings of the First Shared Task on Automatic Minuting at Interspeech*, 2021:1–8.

Thomas Wolf, Lysandre Debut, Victor Sanh, Julien Chaumond, Clement Delangue, Anthony Moi, Pierric Cistac, Tim Rault, Rémi Louf, Morgan Funtowicz, Joe Davison, Sam Shleifer, Patrick von Platen, Clara Ma, Yacine Jernite, Julien Plu, Canwen Xu, Teven Le Scao, Sylvain Gugger, Mariama Drame, Quentin Lhoest, and Alexander M. Rush. 2019. Huggingface's transformers: State-of-the-art natural language processing.

Zhou Zhao, Haojie Pan, Changjie Fan, Yan Liu, Linlin Li, Min Yang, and Deng Cai. 2019. Abstractive meeting summarization via hierarchical adaptive segmental network learning. In *The World Wide Web Conference*, WWW '19, page 3455–3461, New York, NY, USA. Association for Computing Machinery.

A Example

This is an example of our model's output on the testset:
instance: The_Simpsons_388
summary: PERSON0, Bart and Lisa are making pancakes for Mom's birthday. They also got her a bottle of French perfume from gay Paree for her birthday. It's a surprise for Dad. It's Homer Simpson's 34th birthday. He's having dinner with his friends at the Singing Sirloin tonight. Marge's mother has not opened her birthday present yet. PERSON1 got a bowling ball as a present from PERSON3. She's not very good at it, so she's going to use it. PERSON4 gives her a paper with a score on it and a pair of shoes. Marge writes down the score on a PERSON1, Marge, Homer, Lisa, Bart and Maggie are learning how to play the game. It costs forty dollars for the lessons. PERSON1 and Marge are going to meet for brunch tomorrow. Marge is going bowling again tonight. PERSON10 is giving her a bowling lesson. Marge is in a restaurant. She is dancing with Jacques. PERSON13 and PERSON13 are angry at their father for not listening to their advice. Bart and Lisa are afraid something is wrong with their father. Marge made a peanut butter and jelly sandwich for PERSON3. He eats it. He is going to the backseat of

Mapping: "LISA": "PERSON0",
"MARGE": "PERSON1",
"WAITERS": "PERSON2",
"HOMER": "PERSON3",
"MANAGER": "PERSON4",
"LENNY": "PERSON5",
"SELMA": "PERSON6",
"HELEN": "PERSON7",
"VOICE": "PERSON8",
"COWORKER": "PERSON9",
"JACQUES": "PERSON10",
"PATTY": "PERSON11",
"MAN": "PERSON12",
"BART": "PERSON13",
"LISA + BART": "PERSON14",
"COP": "PERSON15"

Long Input Dialogue Summarization with Sketch Supervision for Summarization of Primetime Television Transcripts

Nataliia Kees
inovex GmbH
nataliia.kees@inovex.de

Thien Quang Nguyen
Technical University of Munich
thien.nguyen@tum.de

Tobias Eder
Technical University of Munich
tobias.eder@in.tum.de

Georg Groh
Technical University of Munich
grohg@in.tum.de

Abstract

This paper presents our entry to the CreativeSumm 2022 shared task, tackling the problem of prime-time television screenplay summarization based on the SummScreen Forever Dreaming dataset. Our approach utilizes extended Longformers combined with sketch supervision including categories specifically for scene descriptions. Our system was able to produce the shortest summaries out of all submissions. While some problems with factual consistency still remain, the system was scoring highest among competitors in the ROUGE and BERTScore evaluation categories.

1 Introduction

This paper represents our submission to the CreativeSumm 2022 shared task, which itself was subdivided into four distinct summarization tasks and consists of summarization of (i) chapters from novels, (ii) movie scripts, (iii) prime time television scrips and (iv) day-time television scripts. Our system focused on summarizing prime-time television show transcripts for task (iii) and aims at producing a brief description for a single episode of its main developments based on the underlying episode script.

Our system has been trained on the SummScreen Forever Dreaming (FD) dataset (Chen et al., 2022) that was released as part of the shared task to produce automatic abstractive summaries of TV show screenplays. The structure of the data and its strong stylistic reliance on dialogues allows us to construct the problem of TV screenplay summarization as a dialogue summarization problem. To solve this, we use a dialogue summarization architecture of Abstractive Dialogue Summarization with Sketch Supervision introduced by Wu et al. (2021) as a base architecture and adjust it to process large inputs of up to 16384 tokens and handle scene descriptions, which is one important characteristic of this data and makes it different from typical dialogue data.

With our architecture, we achieve results which strongly outperform the baseline end-to-end models and result in better performance than our competitors on word- and context-based metrics on the CreativeSumm 2022 shared task.

2 Related Work

2.1 Dialogue Summarization

Existing research in dialogue summarization is of high relevance for our task, since we approach the task of summarizing TV screenplay transcripts as dialogue summarization and are interested in state-of-the-art methods which would be suitable for the given dataset. In this chapter, we present a few approaches we considered for using to solve the task of television screenplay summarization.

There have been several works achieving some progress in producing dialogue summaries (e.g. Chen and Yang, 2020, Liu et al., 2021, Wu et al., 2021, Liu and Chen, 2021, Zou et al., 2021, Park and Lee, 2022). Because dialogues, especially in the context of television show scripts, can be analyzed from different perspectives (e.g. topics they cover or order of the utterances, or stages of the discussion they represent), an interesting approach in this regard has been presented by Chen and Yang (2020). They model conversations via these different standpoints, which they call *views*, by incorporating different structures a conversation can consist of, and use those for summarization. Chen and Yang (2020) distinguish between different views, which focus on a specific aspect of each speaker's intent. For instance, one view would structure the conversation around topics, whereas another view would focus on the order of the utterances. The authors segment conversations according to the views into single blocks of utterances. That way, they extract relevant information for different contexts and intents in order to generate summaries. For the summary generation they apply a conversation encoder

Proceedings of the 58th Annual Meeting of the Association for Computational Linguistics, pages 29–35
July 5–10, 2020. ©2020 Association for Computational Linguistics
https://doi.org/10.26615/978-954-452-056-4_005

consisting of a combination of BART (Lewis et al., 2019) and LSTM layers and a multi-view decoder which is built with transformer layers (Vaswani et al., 2017), combining the views.

A specific characteristic of dialogues is the fact that all relevant information is scattered across utterances and it might be hard to connect the pieces of the discourse in an automated way. To tackle the scatteredness of information across all utterances, Liu et al. (2021) use the notion of *coreferences*, which they use to gather relevant parts of information across multiple segments in a conversation. They introduce a dataset with annotations of the coreferences, which rely on coreference resolution models, and use graph convolutional neural networks on graph representations of the conversations and their coreferences. To obtain a contextualized representation of the nodes, the authors introduce coreference-guided self-attention to the coreference information.

Another approach, which aims at tackling both the scatteredness of information and the distinctions between single logical blocks of the discourse flow in a dialogue, is the *Controllable Abstractive Dialogue Summarization (CODS)* architecture by Wu et al. (2021). In addition to that, it aims at controlling the length of the output summary, which is particularly interesting in the context of long dialogue summarization, where the possibilities with regard to the output summary length are broad. The approach envisions the generation of a summary sketch of the dialogue and using a segmentation model to control the amount of sentences the model generates for the summary (Wu et al., 2021). The sketch contains only the most relevant information, therefore excluding non-factual sentences. It outlines the intents of each speaker and contains the key phrases representing these intents. It also functions as a weakly supervised signal for the model. The length control takes place via predicting the text span cutoffs, which lead to multiple segments as an output. The more sentences the model is supposed to generate, the more segments will be extracted. Of all three architectures, Wu et al. (2021) report for their CODS model the highest performance on SAMSum data (Gliwa et al., 2019)[1]. This, along with the convenient use of the intent model, which can be expanded easily, is the reason why we make use of this model as a basis for our experiments, adjusting it to our data as described in Chapter 4. Though, we do not use the segmentation model in our experiments, as we want to keep the architecture simple and reduce the environmental footprint of the training process. As the authors report, removing the segmentation influences the performance on the SAMSum dataset only marginally (ROUGE-1 F1 of 51.79 for sketch supervision vs. 52.65 for the full CODS approach (Wu et al., 2021)), which can be seen as negligible.

2.2 Summarization of Television Show Transcripts

The SummScreen-FD dataset is a summarization dataset which provides pairs of TV series transcripts and human-written summaries (Chen et al., 2022). One of the challenges it poses is its long input size (see Chapter 3 for details), which requires special treatment due to high computation complexity of typical transformer models.

Zhang et al. (2021) compare several methods on the SummScreen-FD dataset, such as BART (Lewis et al., 2019) with input length of 1024 tokens, HMNet (Zhu et al., 2020), which is a hierarchical model for dialogue summarization, with input size of 8192 tokens, as well as Longformer Encoder-Decoder (Beltagy et al., 2020) with input size of 4096 tokens. They also compare these to a retrieve-then-summarize pipeline based on TF-IDF, BM25 or Locator (Zhong et al., 2021) retriever and arrive at the conclusion that a BART-large model (Lewis et al., 2019) pretrained on CNN/DM dataset yields the best performance on SummScreen-FD, achieving a ROUGE-1 F1 score of 28.86.

Zhang et al. (2022) approach summarization of long-input dialogues by using a greedy segment-then-combine method for compressing the inputs and use two summarizers based on BART (Lewis et al., 2019): one produces coarse summaries and another one (with different parameters) finegrains the coarse summarizes to produce the final outputs. They report reaching 32.48 in terms of ROUGE-1 score on SummScreen-FD data.

Because of the potentially different data splits that the authors of the above models have used for their evaluation, which most probably do not correspond to the blind test set the CreativeSumm workshop participants received for the shared task, these numbers are not directly comparable with our evaluation results reported in Chapter 5. However, they are useful as an orientation of the minimal

[1] Reported ROUGE-1 F1 score of 52.65 for CODS (Wu et al., 2021) compared to 50.9 for Coref (Liu et al., 2021) and 49.3 for MultiView (Chen and Yang, 2020)

expected performance for our selected approach.

3 Dataset

The SummScreen dataset contains television show screenplays – one screenplay per episode – and human-written summaries which provide a short description of the story line of the given episode (Chen et al., 2022). It consists of two parts: SummScreen Forever Dreaming (FD), which contains prime TV shows screenplays, and SummScreen TV Megasite (TMS), consisting of daytime TV show screenplays.

In this work, we focus on SummScreen-FD as our data source for model training and evaluation. Our training data contains 4008 instances of TV series episodes with corresponding hand-written summaries as gold labels, for validation we use additional 337 instances and for testing 459 examples. An example snippet from the dataset can be found in Table 1.

An important characteristic of this data is that the input length of the screenplays much exceeds the typical input length that standard Transformer-based language models are designed to tackle: in terms of word count our train data, for example, has on average 7587 words, with a smallest screenplay having 1934 words and the longest one 21435 words. Outputs in the training data are much shorter, with average of 111 words, where the longest summary has 822 words and the shortest summary being only 8 words long. This requires an approach which would be capable of processing large inputs, grasping temporal relations and references on long distances, and squeezing them into concise outputs.

Such large input size can in part be attributed to another characteristic of SummScreen-FD, which makes it different from SummScreen-TMS, which is that it also contains descriptions about environments or characters and their feelings, similar to scene setting descriptions. We exploit this characteristic in our method, as we describe in more detail in Chapter 4.

4 Method

To tackle the task of summarizing TV show screenplays, we construct it as a dialogue summarization problem and use a dialogue summarization model proposed by Wu et al. (2021). Before processing the dialogues, a preprocessing pipeline also provided by the authors is applied, which first

Leo: Piper?
Piper: Hm?
Leo: What are you doing?
(Leo sits up. Piper walks out of the nursery carrying a packet of diapers.)
Piper: I'm putting the diapers back where they belong, that is what I'm doing.
(She puts the diapers on a shelf.)

Table 1: Example of a screenplay snippet from SummScreen-FD with environment or character descriptions (in brackets)

cleans up the text and labels the utterances based on whether they have meaningful overlap with tokens from the gold labels or not, based on the intersection of their stemmed tokens. Meaningful overlap here means at least one hit which is not an English stopword.

As mentioned in Section 2.1, this method introduces the idea of constructing a summary sketch as a step prior to predicting the summary itself, which is one of the main features of this architecture. The summary sketch consists of the keywords extracted by applying syntax-driven sentence compression method (Xu and Durrett, 2019) combined with constituency parsing with a self-attentive encoder (Kitaev and Klein, 2018), as implemented in the Berkeley Neural Parser[2]. The relations between the keywords are modelled according to a predefined *utterance intent classification* model (Wu et al., 2021). This idea makes this method suitable to our long inputs and intricate conversation structures with scene breaks and important information spread over several not necessarily adjacent utterances, because it helps capture only the core information, excluding the character or plot development turns, irrelevant to the summaries.

This dialogue processing pipeline is also easily adjustable due to the flexibility of the predefined utterance intent model. In the original model, the summary sketches are built after the FIVE Ws principle, classifying the utterances as to their intent of „why“, „what“, „where“, „when“ or „confirm“. Utterances which do not fall under any of these categories are marked as „abstain“. We extend this approach by incorporating the scene setting information by introducing the additional intent of „scene“. Subsequently, in our pipeline we create summary sketches based on the intent information

[2]https://spacy.io/universe/project/self-attentive-parser

for each line from the transcripts and the keywords which could be identified, removing noise from the data (see Tables 2 and 3 for examples). We limit the amount of utterances which are considered as a part of the sketch to 20 in order to stay below the maximum output limit of 1024 tokens.

intent	line	keywords
abstain	*Leo:* Piper?	['piper']
abstain	*Piper:* Hm?	[]
what	*Leo:* What are you doing?	[]
scene	(Leo sits up. Piper walks out of the nursery carrying a packet of diapers.)	['leo', 'piper']
abstain	*Piper:* I'm putting the diapers back where they belong, that is what I'm doing.	[]
scene	(She puts the diapers on a shelf.)	[]
abstain	*Leo:* But it's 2:00 in the morning.	[]
what	*Piper:* Yeah, well, apparently our little ghosts and goblins are not sleeping, so how can I? I wish they would just attack us rather than move stuff around.	['are not sleeping']
scene	(She goes back in the nursery and picks up a pile of diapers from under the crib. She takes them into the bedroom and places them on the shelf.)	['takes them into the bedroom and places them on the shelf']

Table 2: Example of processed dialogues with the classified intent and extracted keywords from SummScreen-FD

The gold label is then concatenated to the sketch separated by the token **TLDR**, which together serve as a label which the generator is trained to predict (for an example, see Table 3). Our generator architecture is based on the Longformer Encoder Decoder (LED) (Beltagy et al., 2020), of which we used the large version with input size of 16384 tokens. The model has been retrieved via the HuggingFace transformers model hub[3]. A graphic representation of our pipeline is in Figure 1.

The training has been performed on a single NVIDIA A40-48C GPU with 48 GB RAM with training batch size of 2 and gradient checkpointing. We performed a few experiments, tuning the learning rate and adjusting the maximum epoch size. We could achieve the fastest and most reliable training process training at initial learning rate of 5e-5 (with Adam optimizer), maximum epoch size of 40. Early stopping ended the training after reaching the best model after 19 training epochs and model not improving for 5 subsequent epochs.

The training script and instructions can be found on Github[4].

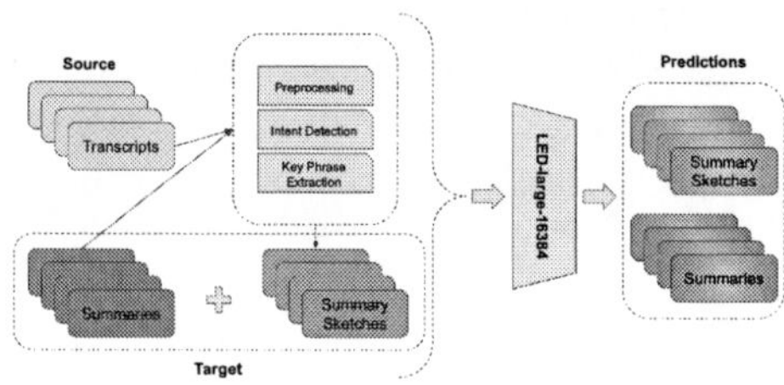

Figure 1: Workflow of the used framework to summarize TV show transcripts. It processes transcripts (source) and gold label summaries, modelling intent of the source and extracting key phrases based on the overlap with the gold summaries, and creates summary sketches (e.g. Table 3) and concatenates them with the summaries, which together serve as model targets. A Longformer Encoder Decoder is then used to predict both summary sketches and summaries from the source.

5 Results

The winning model that we then used for producing summaries for the blind test data was determined based on the validation set performance employing early stopping. We include evaluations of the validation ROUGE-1 and ROUGE-L scores across all training epochs in Figure 2. The best performing model reached a ROUGE-1 performance of 34.45 and ROUGE-L of 28.05 respectively in Epoch 19. Based on this we chose this model for evaluation on the test set.

Test set evaluation shows generally lower, but similarly promising results. Table 4 shows some of the shared task results for reference. Our model was able to beat all LED baselines by a large margin, while simultaneously achieving the highest

[3]https://huggingface.co/allenai/led-large-16384
[4]https://github.com/nkees/creative-abs-summ-sketch

target (sketch + gold label)	prediction
0 abstain lily marshall waits at the airport 1 abstain during the second year of college , when lily is back from vacation marshall 2 none 3 abstain lily marshall waits at the airport 4 where ted 5 none 6 none 7 abstain ted and marshall are in mcclaren's 8 none 9 none 10 abstain lily want me to take a taxi to the airport just to get a taxi in the opposite direction 11 none 12 none 13 abstain that's all i want in the world 14 abstain runs out of the bar ted barney 15 abstain wanted to see what looks like a license in arizona 16 none 17 what 's good 18 none 19 none **TLDR** Lily comes back from a trip to Seattle only to run into a blizzard, which may threaten an airport ritual of meeting Marshall. Meanwhile, Ted & Barney offer to keep watch over the bar at MacLaren's while awaiting their dates, since Carl wants to close up early.	0 none 1 when when lily is back from vacation 2 none 3 none 4 where ted 5 none 6 none 7 abstain are in mcclaren's 8 none 9 none 10 none 11 none 12 abstain that's all i want in the world 13 abstain ted and barney 14 abstain wanted to see what looks like a license in arizona 15 none 16 what 's good 17 none 18 none 19 what barney leads ted to the bar entrance. **TLDR** When Lily is forced to spend the holiday in Seattle with her boyfriend, Ranjit, Ted and Barney try to find a bar.

Table 3: Example of target and prediction, containing concatenated together sketch and summary, for a transcript from SummScreen-FD (from validation split)

Model	ROUGE-1	ROUGE-L	BERTScore-F1	LitePyramid-p2c	SummaC_{ZS}	Length
LED 1024	14.28	12.36	40.52	13.71	05.59	330
LED 4096	16.94	15.01	46.00	03.37	10.52	188
LED 16384	15.14	13.34	44.89	03.37	16.44	192
InoTUM	28.60	25.29	57.50	06.73	02.72	86
Team UFAL	24.69	23.00	52.85	04.72	12.82	289
AMRTVSumm	23.07	21.06	51.08	01.16	02.40	256

Table 4: Abridged test set performance for different metrics across systems in the shared task

scores of the submitted systems in the ROUGE and BERTScore categories. Detailed evaluations compared to the various baselines can be found in Table 4. ROUGE-1 on the test set amounted to 28.60 and ROUGE-L to 25.29. At the same time the system was also able to produce the shortest summaries of all comparison systems, with only an average of 86 tokens per summary, making it less than half as long as any other comparison summary system. Because of the shorter length of the summaries, it is, therefore, not surprising that our system also achieves the highest BERTScore Precision out of all systems at 59.34. More surprising, however, is the great recall performance, which again is the highest out of all submissions at 56.09, demonstrating that conciseness does not necessarily sacrifice relevant information. The simultaneous good results on ROUGE and BERTScore, combined with the shorter length of summaries, makes us confident that the approach we tried warrants further exploration.

The LitePyramid evaluation shows good performance compared to other competitors, but here we are witnessing that our system is not able to outperform the LED_1024 baseline model. Lastly in the $SummaC_{ZS}$ scores our system, unfortunately, scored comparatively low, suggesting problems with factual consistency of the generated outputs. To investigate this problem of factual consistency, we compared outputs of the system manually with reference scripts and found this problem to be true. Thus, improving factual consistency would be a vital step for improving the overall model in the future.

We present an example of the generated summaries of our system in Table 5. The examples taken from the TV Show Breaking Bad are consistent enough to fit the theme of the show and incorporate certain elements of the episodes in question, but tend to mix in information that is not present in the actual script.

The number of utterances that go into the sketch for each script is another hyperparameter, that can be freely set and tuned by the developer. To further explore the effect of the sketches in the overall pipeline we conducted experiments varying the number of utterances for each individual sketch. Utilizing more utterances has however not lead to any significant changes in performance on the dev set. Due to the nature of the shared task, we could

Test set instance	Summary
Breaking_Bad_276	Dr. Bravenec helps Walter decide whether or not to have the lobectomy. After much consideration, Walter decides to go through with it. Meanwhile, after learning the truth from his doctor about the status of his cancer, Dr. Bravenec decides to take action for himself.
Breaking_Bad_290	Walter decides to continue treatment after he receives promising news about his cancer. Meanwhile, Jesse has problems with the new tenant and tries to get Jane to move into her apartment with him.

Table 5: Examples of generated summaries for the TV show Breaking Bad

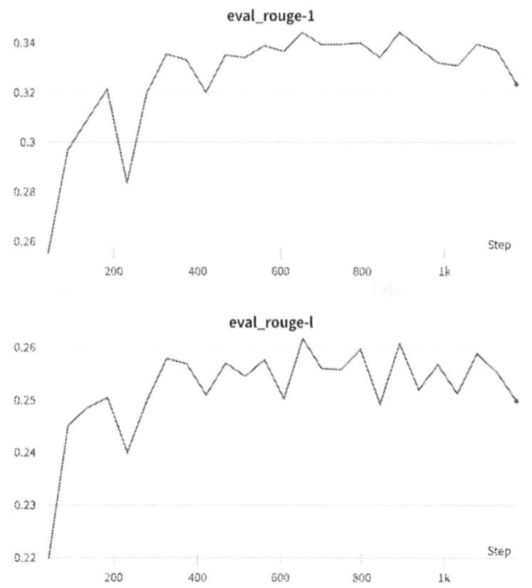

Figure 2: ROUGE-1 and ROUGE-L scores on the validation set across training epochs.

not provide evaluation on the test set, but believe these not to be a deciding factor in the success of the system.

6 Conclusion

In this paper, we presented our submission to the CreativeSumm 2022 shared task for tackling the problem of summarizing television script based on the SummScreen Forever Dreaming dataset. Our system is based on previous work by Wu et al. (2021) and extends the utterance and sketch categories particularly for the task of screenplay summarization. We have shown that this method can improve over baseline LED summarization significantly and have achieved good ROUGE and BERTScore performance, which were the highest among submitted systems. At the same time, this method was able to produce the most concise summaries out of the field.

The biggest issue of our system is factual consistency, often mixing up specific details and actors in the summarization part, thus creating seemingly good summaries but with factual errors, which would be hard to spot without actual knowledge of the underlying text. Improving factual consistency would, therefore, be an important follow-up step in further developing this approach.

Similarly, the preprocessing of sketches could be optimized by reevaluating utterance categories and trying to further specify relevant utterances for the task of script summarization with less of a focus on spoken dialogue alone to improve the base performance even more.

We are confident that with an improvement of the factual consistency our system will be able to also score higher in a human evaluation process, where such discrepancies are weighed much higher than in a pure word-level or representation-level approach.

References

Iz Beltagy, Matthew E. Peters, and Arman Cohan. 2020. Longformer: The long-document transformer. *arXiv:2004.05150.*

Jiaao Chen and Diyi Yang. 2020. Multi-view sequence-to-sequence models with conversational structure for abstractive dialogue summarization. *CoRR*, abs/2010.01672.

Mingda Chen, Zewei Chu, Sam Wiseman, and Kevin Gimpel. 2022. Summscreen: A dataset for abstractive screenplay summarization. In *ACL*.

Bogdan Gliwa, Iwona Mochol, Maciej Biesek, and Aleksander Wawer. 2019. SAMSum corpus: A human-annotated dialogue dataset for abstractive summarization. In *Proceedings of the 2nd Workshop on New Frontiers in Summarization*, pages 70–79, Hong Kong, China. Association for Computational Linguistics.

Nikita Kitaev and Dan Klein. 2018. Constituency parsing with a self-attentive encoder. *CoRR*, abs/1805.01052.

Mike Lewis, Yinhan Liu, Naman Goyal, Marjan Ghazvininejad, Abdelrahman Mohamed, Omer Levy, Veselin Stoyanov, and Luke Zettlemoyer. 2019. BART: denoising sequence-to-sequence pre-training for natural language generation, translation, and comprehension. *CoRR*, abs/1910.13461.

Zhengyuan Liu and Nancy Chen. 2021. Controllable neural dialogue summarization with personal named entity planning. In *Proceedings of the 2021 Conference on Empirical Methods in Natural Language Processing*, pages 92–106, Online and Punta Cana, Dominican Republic. Association for Computational Linguistics.

Zhengyuan Liu, Ke Shi, and Nancy F. Chen. 2021. Coreference-aware dialogue summarization. *CoRR*, abs/2106.08556.

Seongmin Park and Jihwa Lee. 2022. Unsupervised abstractive dialogue summarization with word graphs and POV conversion. In *Proceedings of the 2nd Workshop on Deriving Insights from User-Generated Text*, pages 1–9, (Hybrid) Dublin, Ireland, and Virtual. Association for Computational Linguistics.

Ashish Vaswani, Noam Shazeer, Niki Parmar, Jakob Uszkoreit, Llion Jones, Aidan N. Gomez, Lukasz Kaiser, and Illia Polosukhin. 2017. Attention is all you need. *CoRR*, abs/1706.03762.

Chien-Sheng Wu, Linqing Liu, Wenhao Liu, Pontus Stenetorp, and Caiming Xiong. 2021. Controllable abstractive dialogue summarization with sketch supervision. In *Findings of the Association for Computational Linguistics: ACL-IJCNLP 2021*, pages 5108–5122, Online. Association for Computational Linguistics.

Jiacheng Xu and Greg Durrett. 2019. Neural extractive text summarization with syntactic compression. *CoRR*, abs/1902.00863.

Yusen Zhang, Ansong Ni, Ziming Mao, Chen Henry Wu, Chenguang Zhu, Budhaditya Deb, Ahmed Awadallah, Dragomir Radev, and Rui Zhang. 2022. Summ^n: A multi-stage summarization framework for long input dialogues and documents. In *Proceedings of the 60th Annual Meeting of the Association for Computational Linguistics (Volume 1: Long Papers)*, pages 1592–1604, Dublin, Ireland. Association for Computational Linguistics.

Yusen Zhang, Ansong Ni, Tao Yu, Rui Zhang, Chenguang Zhu, Budhaditya Deb, Asli Celikyilmaz, Ahmed Hassan Awadallah, and Dragomir Radev. 2021. An exploratory study on long dialogue summarization: What works and what's next. In *Findings of the Association for Computational Linguistics: EMNLP 2021*, pages 4426–4433, Punta Cana, Dominican Republic. Association for Computational Linguistics.

Ming Zhong, Da Yin, Tao Yu, Ahmad Zaidi, Mutethia Mutuma, Rahul Jha, Ahmed Hassan Awadallah, Asli Celikyilmaz, Yang Liu, Xipeng Qiu, and Dragomir Radev. 2021. QMSum: A new benchmark for query-based multi-domain meeting summarization. In *Proceedings of the 2021 Conference of the North American Chapter of the Association for Computational Linguistics: Human Language Technologies*, pages 5905–5921, Online. Association for Computational Linguistics.

Chenguang Zhu, Ruochen Xu, Michael Zeng, and Xuedong Huang. 2020. A hierarchical network for abstractive meeting summarization with cross-domain pretraining. In *Findings of the Association for Computational Linguistics: EMNLP 2020*, pages 194–203, Online. Association for Computational Linguistics.

Yicheng Zou, Bolin Zhu, Xingwu Hu, Tao Gui, and Qi Zhang. 2021. Low-resource dialogue summarization with domain-agnostic multi-source pretraining. In *Proceedings of the 2021 Conference on Empirical Methods in Natural Language Processing*, pages 80–91, Online and Punta Cana, Dominican Republic. Association for Computational Linguistics.

AMRTVSumm: AMR-augmented Hierarchical Network for TV Transcript Summarization

Yilun Hua*
Columbia University
yh3228@columbia.edu

Zhaoyuan Deng*
Columbia University
zd2286@columbia.edu

Zhijie Xu
Carnegie Mellon University
zhijiex@andrew.cmu.edu

Abstract

This paper describes our AMRTVSumm system for the SummScreen datasets in the Automatic Summarization for Creative Writing shared task (Creative-Summ 2022). In order to capture the complicated entity interactions and dialogue structures in transcripts of TV series, we introduce a new Abstract Meaning Representation (AMR) (Banarescu et al., 2013), particularly designed to represent individual scenes in an episode. We also propose a new cross-level cross-attention mechanism to incorporate these scene AMRs into a hierarchical encoder-decoder baseline. On both the ForeverDreaming and TVMegaSite datasets of SummScreen, our system consistently outperforms the hierarchical transformer baseline. Compared with the state-of-the-art DialogLM (Zhong et al., 2021), our system still has a lower performance primarily because it is pretrained only on out-of-domain news data, unlike DialogLM, which uses extensive in-domain pretraining on dialogue and TV show data. Overall, our work suggests a promising direction to capture complicated long dialogue structures through graph representations and the need to combine graph representations with powerful pretrained language models.

1 Introduction

Abstractive summarization of TV show episodes aims to produce a summary from their transcripts or screenplays, capturing important plot development and character relations. For this shared task, we participated in the two SummScreen categories, which involve abstractively summarizing prime-time TV series (ForeverDreaming) and daytime soap operas (TVMegaSite) (Chen et al., 2022). This task presents several new challenges compared with other abstractive summarization tasks. First, transformer-based language models that perform well on shorter texts become computationally expensive when their self-attention is applied to long inputs (Vaswani et al., 2017). Also, consecutive scenes often describe parallel or different subplots, making it difficult to integrate information and present a correct narrative (Chen et al., 2022). Finally, like other dialogue texts such as meetings and media interviews, TV transcripts contain complicated character and entity interactions as well as more varied structures.

Works on long-document summarization have explored transformers with sparse or window-based attention (Beltagy et al., 2020; Wang et al., 2020), hierarchical models (Zhu et al., 2020), and the "retrieve-then-summarize" approach (Chen et al., 2022; Zhang et al., 2021). Large pretrained language models such as BART-large also give strong results by taking longer inputs at the cost of larger embeddings and increased computational complexity (Lewis et al., 2019; Zhong et al., 2021). However, despite the many works addressing the long transcript problem, few have studied novel approaches to model the complicated interactions and structures in TV transcripts. Even the state-of-the-art on SummScreen, DialogLM, relies on dialogue-specific denoising pretraining on TV data. The model architecture itself does not address TV transcripts' conversational structures and takes the input transcripts as plain texts (Zhong et al., 2021).

Therefore, we propose a novel Abstract Meaning Representation (AMR) to capture the diverse entity interactions and complex structures of TV transcripts. AMR, as a graph representation, captures the most salient semantic knowledge using its concept nodes and preserves inter-concept relations with its labeled edges. It is thus believed to convey information orthogonal to the text input (Song et al., 2019). Our work generalizes the sentence-level AMR introduced by Banarescu et al. (2013), adding new features to make them suitable for individual scenes of TV shows. We use these scene-level AMRs to augment a hierarchical

*equal contribution

Proceedings of the 58th Annual Meeting of the Association for Computational Linguistics, pages 36–43
July 5–10, 2020. ©2020 Association for Computational Linguistics
https://doi.org/10.26615/978-954-452-056-4_006

encoder-decoder baseline. To this end, we also propose a cross-level cross-attention to scene AMRs, such that the encoder of local tokens and utterance embeddings can benefit from the structural information and higher-level semantics from the entire corresponding scene, without being interfered by an adjacent scene, which may focus on a parallel or different subplot.

To sum up, the major contributions of our work are presented as follows:

- We propose the steps to construct scene AMRs and introduce 1) Speaker/Utterance nodes and 2) Coreference/Pronoun edges, both of which connect the standard sentence AMRs to capture and extract core semantic and structural information of a scene.
- We design a cross-level cross-attention mechanism so that the encoding of local tokens and utterance embeddings can benefit from the structural and higher-level information from the scene.
- We demonstrate the effectiveness of our AMR augmentation on SummScreen and discuss the need to combine it with dialogue-specific pretraining.

2 Datasets

We participated in the two SummScreen categories of the CreativeSumm 2022 shared task: summarization of primetime television transcripts (ForeverDreaming) and summarization of daytime "soap opera" transcripts (TVMegaSite) (Chen et al., 2022).

We primarily experimented with our system on ForeverDreaming, since it includes more genres and covers 66 TV shows in the train set. We used its entire train set of 3673 episodes to train our model. For TVMegaSite, we only used 6000 of its 18915 training episodes due to the time constraint. The 6000-episode subset was sampled from the original train set to include approximately the same number of episodes from each TV show. We still use the original dev and test sets for both ForeverDreaming and TVMegaSite.

3 Constructing AMR Representation For TV Series

3.1 Scene AMRs

A scene in a TV show episode is a consecutive sequence of closely related lines and actions. For TV transcripts, in particular, we define a scene as a sequence of character utterances and stage directions contributing to a subplot. Here, an utterance is an uninterrupted line by a character, which can contain one or more sentences. Within a scene, speakers may respond to each other, request and perform actions, and refer to entities mentioned by others. All of these interactions give rise to complex dialogue structures. Therefore, we use the AMR graph representation to explicitly capture these important relations and core semantics, which can be difficult to discern for conventional transformers operating on text input.

To construct scene AMRs, we adapt the steps in Bai et al. (2021), which build dialogue AMRs, and additionally introduce speaker nodes, utterance nodes, and a new procedure to represent coreferences. As illustrated by Figure 1, given a scene consisting of multiple utterances, we use the AMR parser by Cai and Lam (2020) to obtain an AMR graph for each utterance and then construct the scene AMR by connecting utterance AMRs. We then add utterance nodes, speaker nodes, and a dummy scene node (the root node), as well as the edges that capture node relations.

Utterance Node/ Utterance Edge. Given an utterance containing one or more sentences, we parse each sentence into its AMR graphs, and connect them with an utterance node tagged `utter` through sentence edges (tagged as `snt1`, `snt2`, etc.). We then connect the utterance node to the corresponding speaker node with an utterance edge (tagged as `utter1`, `utter2`, etc.).

Speaker Node/ Participant Edge. For each speaker in the scene, we add a speaker node tagged with the corresponding speaker name and connect it with the scene node using a participant edge (tagged as `participant1`, `participant2`, etc.). The scene node therefore acts as a root of the entire scene AMR.

Compared with Bai et al. (2021), we want our proposed speaker nodes and utterance nodes to encode the fine-grained hierarchical information from different levels of the scene AMR (synthesizing multiple utterances by one speaker, multiple sentences within one utterance, and etc.). This is made possible by our graph encoder, which exploits their abundant and unique interactions with other AMR concepts (see Section 4.1).

Coreference Edge. Like Bai et al. (2021), we

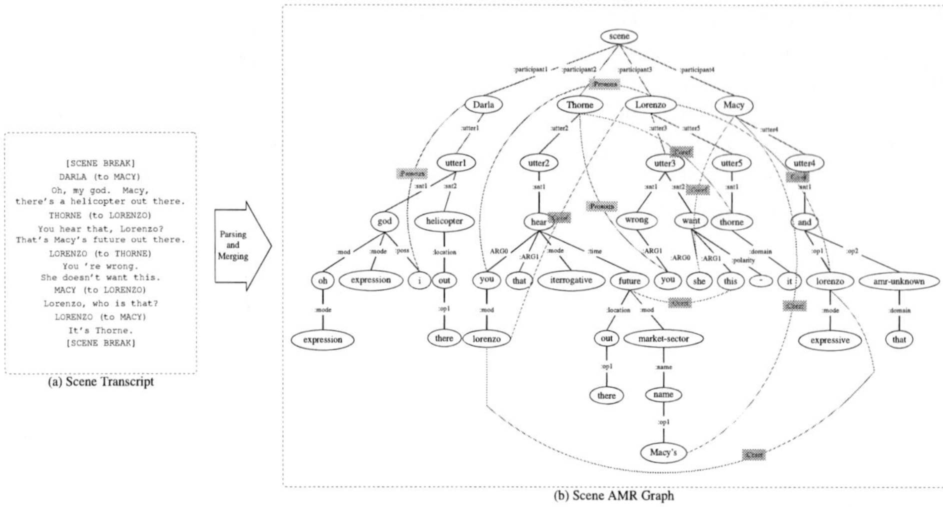

(a) Scene Transcript

(b) Scene AMR Graph

Figure 1: Generating Scene AMR

use NeuralCoref[1] to obtain coreference relations between words, and JAMR[2] to obtain alignment between concepts and words. Yet unlike Bai et al. (2021), if an utterance mentions a speaker (often a third character), we also connect their concept in utterance AMR to the corresponding speaker node.

Pronoun Edge. Because the off-the-shelf NeuralCoref does not guarantee finding all coreference relationships, we also add rule-based pronoun edges. We connect first-person pronoun concepts (e.g., ‘I’, ‘We’) to the current speaker node with pronoun edges. For some TV series, there is information that indicates which character the current speaker is talking to (e.g., Alice (to Bob):). When this information is available, we also connect the second-person pronouns (e.g., ‘You’) to the corresponding speaker node (e.g., Bob).

3.2 Scene Segmentation

Transcripts in the SummScreen dataset often have accurate [SCENE_BREAK] tokens suggesting the beginning of a new scene. These [SCENE_BREAK]s segment the transcripts into texts of reasonable length, for which we can concisely construct scene AMRs and encode them with a graph transformer. However, SummScreen is based on community-contributed transcripts and some of the transcribers may have a different understanding of scene breaks. We found that some episodes contain much fewer [SCENE_BREAK]s than others or no [SCENE_BREAK]s at all.

[1]https://github.com/huggingface/neuralcoref

[2]https://github.com/jflanigan/jamr

Thus, we adopt an existing strategy (Chen and Yang, 2020) that combines the classic topic segment algorithm C99 (Choi, 2000) with SentenceBERT (Reimers and Gurevych, 2019), to re-segment scenes into reasonable lengths. We still primarily use the [SCENE_BREAK]s from the transcripts and only apply this algorithm on long scenes that exceed our threshold of 600 tokens.

4 System Overview

Our AMR-augmented hierarchical summarization network consists of a hierarchical text encoder and a scene-level AMR encoder. The system is illustrated in Figure 2.

4.1 Scene AMR Encoder

The scene-level AMR graphs contain rich structural information and entity interactions in their AMR concepts (nodes) and edges. To exploit this graph information, we apply Zhu et al. (2019)’s structure-aware graph transformer to encode the scene AMRs. Depth-first traversal is used to linearize the AMR into a sequence of concepts. The relationship r_{ij} between a concept pair x_i, x_j is encoded using convolutional network, which convolves the shortest sequence of edges between the pair. As in Zhu et al. (2019), every concept node attends to every other concept node with a modified attention mechanism informed by the relationships between them. In the end, the output of the AMR encoder is

scene-encoder $(scene\_AMR) = \{x_0^c, .., x_m^c\}$, for a scene with m AMR concepts. Note that the

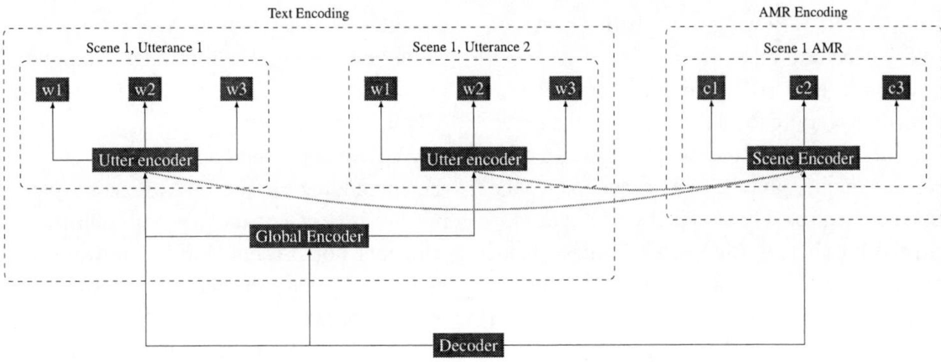

Figure 2: AMR-augmented hierarchical summarization network. The orange arrows indicate the cross-level cross-attention from the utter-encoder's [BOU] outputs to the scene encoder's concept outputs.

graph encoder processes each scene AMR independently, so the encoding of local concepts is not interfered by concepts in neighboring scenes that develop their distinct subplots.

4.2 Hierarchical Text Encoder

We adopt a hierarchical model for the text input because the conventional transformers face huge limitations when encoding long transcripts from TV series. They apply full self-attention to the entire input sequence, despite the computational complexity being quadratic in the input length. Our model adapts the more efficient hierarchical architecture from HMNet (Zhu et al., 2020), which has shown promising results on meetings and other long-dialogue summarization tasks.

Utterance-level Encoder. Following Zhu et al. (2020), our hierarchical structure starts with an utterance-level transformer (utter-encoder), which encodes a sequence of tokens from an utterance u_i using self-attention. We initialize a trainable token embedding matrix D using the pre-trained weights from Zhu et al. (2020). Following their approach, we enrich the token representations by training two other embedding matrices for part-of-speech (POS) and entity tags. The token embedding, POS embedding, and entity embedding are concatenated into the overall token input $x_{i,j}$ (for the j-th token in the i-th utterance). A special token $w_{i,0}$=[BOU] (beginning-of-utterance) is added before every utterance, which is essential for the later utterance representation and cross-attention. We denote the utterance-level encoding operation in every transformer layer as follows:

layer-k$(\{\hat{x}_{i,0,k}, .., \hat{x}_{i,L_i,k}\})$

$= \{\hat{x}_{i,0,k+1}, .., \hat{x}_{i,L_i,k+1}\}$, for the i-th utterance that has length L_i.

Cross-level Cross-attention to AMR outputs. The [BOU] token we added above is analogous to the [BOS] (beginning-of-sentence) token in document encoders. Conventionally, the hidden state output for the [BOS] token can be trained to directly model sentence-level information. For dialogues, however, an utterance has many diverse and complicated structures, making it more difficult to derive reliable patterns through self-attention. Therefore, we enrich the [BOU] embedding $\hat{x}_{i,0,k+1}$ with the scene AMR. In an utterance-level encoder layer, the [BOU] embedding will first have full attention to the tokens in the same utterance. It then cross-attends to the hidden states of all AMR concepts from the entire scene where this utterance locates. Specifically, we derive the Key and Value matrices for the cross-attention from the AMR hidden states and the Query matrix from the [BOU] embeddings.

We call this mechanism "cross-level" cross-attention because it allows the upper-level, more global information (scene-level) to guide the encoding of lower-level information (utterance-level). First, it improves the utterance representation by providing access to the entire scene. Each [BOU] embedding can attend to all the concepts in the scene. Also, the root node, utterance nodes, and important entity nodes, would likely have aggregated information to different extents in graph hidden states so the cross-attention can easily utilize. This scene-level information improves the [BOU] embedding and can guide the extraction of local token features after the improved [BOU] embedding is sent to the next utter-encoder layer. Second, this cross-attention captures the relational information from AMRs, allowing for a better grasp of dialogues' structural features.

This cross-level cross-attention is more efficient than directly attending to all the tokens in the scene. AMR extracts salient features and complex interactions while compressing the input sequence for the attention mechanism. For a typical scene in SummScreen, the number of AMR nodes ranges from half to two-thirds of the token number, leading to significantly lower cross-attention complexity than attending to all the tokens in the scene.

Finally, the overall utter-encoder with cross-level cross-attention has the following operations:

layer-1$(\{x_{i,0}, ..., x_{i,L_i}\})$=$\{\hat{x}_{i,0,1}, ..., \hat{x}_{i,L_i,1}\}$,
layer-k $(\{\hat{x}_{i,0,k}, .., \hat{x}_{i,L_i,k}\})$
$=\{\hat{x}_{i,0,k+1}, .., \hat{x}_{i,L_i,k+1}\}$.

The cross-attention is applied to $\hat{x}_{i,0,k}$ after every layer's self-attention, where $\{x^c_0, ..., x^c_m\}$ is the graph hidden states of the scene:

$\hat{x}_{i,0,k}$ = cross_attn $(\hat{x}_{i,0,k}, \{x^c_0, ..., x^c_m\})$

Overall, the output is:

utter-encoder $(utter_i, \{x^c_0, ..., x^c_m\})$
$= \{x^u_{i,0}, .., x^u_{i,L_i}\}$.

Global Encoder. Like in Zhu et al. (2020), a global transformer aggregates the last utter-encoder hidden states of the [BOU] tokens. The output is denoted as

global-encoder $(\{x^u_{1,0}, .., x^u_{n,0}\}) = \{x^G_1, ..., x^G_n\}$
for an episode of n utterances.

4.3 Decoder

We use a transformer decoder to generate the summary sequence. At each decoding stage t, self-attention is applied to hidden states of the previous $t-1$ generated tokens. Then, the model synthesizes information across different levels by three cross-attention blocks, to the token embeddings from the utter-encoder, to the concept embeddings from the scene-encoder, and to the utterance embeddings from the global-encoder, respectively. In this way, AMR information not only benefits the token and utterance encoding but also directly contributes to the generation of summaries at the decoding stage.

5 Implementation Details

5.1 Initialization

We use the pre-trained weights from Zhu et al. (2020)'s HMNet to initialize our utter-encoder and global-encoder, including the token embedding matrix D. Their pre-training was done on news articles reformatted into conversation-like texts. We consider this an out-of-domain pretraining, which should be distinguished from the dialogue-specific pretraining of the current SOTA system DialogLM (Zhong et al., 2021).

We then copy and resize the matrix D to D_c as the embedding matrix for AMR concepts, expanding the matrix vocabulary with additional AMR concepts not present during pretraining. Since many AMR concepts are also common words and names, initializing with HMNet's pretrained embedding will help better extract relations between text tokens and AMR concepts. However, we do not tie the weights of AMR and text embedding matrices, as we expect them to emphasize different meanings when a token is treated as a word versus as an AMR concept.

5.2 Training

We use an effective batch size of 40 episodes and train our system for 2400 updates. The initial learning rate is set to 5e-6. Within 150 updates, it linearly increases to and remains at 5e-4. In addition, we use RAdam optimizer with $\beta_1 = 0.9$, $\beta_2 = 0.999$.

6 Results

At the time of our blind test submission to the shared task, we only trained our system on smaller subsets of the SummScreen datasets. The resulting checkpoints therefore did not achieve a high performance on the original test sets of SummScreen nor on the blind test sets provided by the shared task. We will analyze these results in Section 6.3. Here, we first present our more recent results from training on the expanded train sets after our blind test submission. Specifically, we eventually used the complete train set for ForeverDreaming and a re-sampled 6000-episode subset for TVMegaSite. All results were reported on the original test sets without re-sampling.

6.1 Results on Original SummScreen Datasets

We primarily compare our results with the hierarchical baseline HMNet from Zhu et al. (2020). After grid searching over key hyper-parameters, we trained HMNet using the same setup as our system, which produced a better result than the setup in the original paper. We also include results of other strong baselines reported by Zhong et al. (2021), including Longformer (Beltagy et al., 2020), BART-Large (Lewis et al., 2019), UNI-LM (Dong et al.,

Models	ForeverDreaming			TVMegaSite		
	R-1	R-2	R-L	R-1	R-2	R-L
Longformer*	25.90	4.20	23.80	42.90	11.90	41.60
BART-Large*	33.82	7.48	29.07	43.54	10.31	41.35
UNILM-base*	32.16	5.93	27.27	43.42	9.62	41.19
DialogLM-sparse*	35.75	8.27	30.76	45.58	10.75	43.31
HMNet	27.08	5.41	23.95	41.04	9.28	39.05
AMR_cross (our system)	31.45	7.39	27.14	43.08	10.77	41.53
- cross attention	31.07	6.15	27.30	-	-	-
- speaker/utter	31.10	6.09	27.26	-	-	-

Table 1: Comparison with baselines and ablation results. * indicates results reported by Zhong et al. (2021). "-" indicates we removed that feature for ablation study.

2019), and DialogLM (Zhong et al., 2021).

As shown in Table 1, our system consistently outperforms its hierarchical baseline HMNet on both ForeverDreaming and TVMegaSite. It also fully outperforms Longformer on ForeverDreaming and achieved comparable results on TVMegaSite, despite using a smaller TVMegaSite train set. In addition, our system sometimes outperformed BART-Large and UNILM-base in Rouge-2 or Rouge-L or both.

Here, HMNet, Longformer, UNILM, and BART-Large are all pretrained on out-of-domain data like our system. This suggests that scene AMR can effectively contribute to a summarization system through cross-attention. However, our system's performance is still lower than that of dialogLM_sparse, one of the best performing dialogLM variants, which uses extensive pretraining on TV data. Therefore, our future work will extend our proposed AMR and cross-attention approaches to combine with more powerful pretrained models.

6.2 Ablation Studies

We used ForeverDreaming to perform ablation studies because it has more TV show genres than TVMegaSite but fewer episodes overall. This allows us to conduct experiments efficiently and obtain more generalizable results. Our ablation includes removing the speaker and utterance nodes and omitting the cross-level cross attention to AMR concepts. Due to the time constraint, we did not perform a separate ablation for the coreference/pronoun edges. For each experiment, we report the ROUGE scores on the original test split of ForeverDreaming.

As shown in the last three lines of Table 1, removing cross attention and speaker/utter nodes both resulted in a lower overall performance than AMR_cross, though they are still better than the HMNet baseline that uses no AMR at all. Part of the performance decrease when speaker nodes are omitted may also come from the loss of coref/pronoun edges associated with these nodes. Therefore, we will conduct more thorough ablation experiments in the future, considering the case when only speaker-associated coref/pronoun edges are removed versus the case when all these edges are removed. Overall, these results suggest the effectiveness of our proposed approaches.

6.3 Blind Test Submission

At the time of blind test submission, we used a model checkpoint trained on a subset of 2000 episodes for ForeverDreaming. For TVMegaSite, we used a subset of 2500 episodes. Table 2 shows that blind test sets seem to be harder than the original test sets: the same model checkpoint achieved 28.84 Rouge-1 for ForeverDreaming's original test set while the Rouge-1 on the blind test was 23.07. The performance drop for TVMegaSite was even greater, from 41.16 Rouge-1 to 34.26 Rouge-1. Other Rouge scores were also lower for the blind test sets. This performance decline was much greater than what we observed between the original train, dev, and test sets in our experiments. This is likely a result of different TV show distributions or different transcript styles between the blind tests and the originally released train/dev/test sets. Using a smaller train set might have undermined our model's generalization, but it is likely not the main reason behind this discrepancy.

Instead, the effects of using smaller train sets are

Data Split	ForeverDreaming			TVMegaSite		
	R-1	R-2	R-L	R-1	R-2	R-L
Blind Test	23.07	3.03	21.06	34.26	7.17	32.80
Original Test	28.84	5.83	25.58	41.16	10.67	39.74

Table 2: Blind test scores vs. original test scores of the checkpoints we used for blind test submission. The original test scores here are lower than those in Table 1 since they come from checkpoints trained on smaller datasets.

most salient when comparing the results in Table 1 and those in Table 2. Our system achieved higher test Rouge scores for both ForeverDreaming and TVMegaSite in Table 1, using checkpoints trained on more data. It suggests that our system responds well to increased dataset sizes, and our future work should exploit all the data available.

7 Conclusion

We describe our AMRTVSumm system for the two SummScreen datasets in the CreativeSumm 2022 shared task. Based on our proposed scene AMR graph and hierarchical architecture with cross-level cross-attention, our system achieves substantial improvement over its hierarchical baseline under the same out-of-domain pretraining. However, it still does not outperform the state-of-the-art model that relies on extensive in-domain pretraining. Our work suggests that despite graph representation's power in modeling complicated dialogue structures, it does not replace the role of dialogue-specific and TV-specific pretraining. A promising future direction will be to leverage the advantages of both by augmenting a state-of-the-art pretrained language model with scene AMRs.

8 Acknowledgements

This work is supported in part by Columbia University under the Class of 1939, Columbia College Summer Research Fellowship. The authors would like to thank Daniel Bauer for his constructive feedback and comments on the use of AMR. The authors are also grateful to Samantha Mayers, Zheyu Liu, Duaa Tariq, António Câmara, and Zongmin Yin for their advice and assistance.

References

Xuefeng Bai, Yulong Chen, Linfeng Song, and Yue Zhang. 2021. Semantic Representation for Dialogue Modeling. In *Proceedings of the 59th Annual Meeting of the Association for Computational Linguistics and the 11th International Joint Conference on Natural Language Processing (Volume 1: Long Papers)*, pages 4430–4445, Online. Association for Computational Linguistics.

Laura Banarescu, Claire Bonial, Shu Cai, Madalina Georgescu, Kira Griffitt, Ulf Hermjakob, Kevin Knight, Philipp Koehn, Martha Palmer, and Nathan Schneider. 2013. Abstract Meaning Representation for sembanking. In *Proceedings of the 7th Linguistic Annotation Workshop and Interoperability with Discourse*, pages 178–186, Sofia, Bulgaria. Association for Computational Linguistics.

Iz Beltagy, Matthew E. Peters, and Arman Cohan. 2020. Longformer: The long-document transformer. *CoRR*, abs/2004.05150.

Deng Cai and Wai Lam. 2020. AMR parsing via graph-sequence iterative inference. In *Proceedings of the 58th Annual Meeting of the Association for Computational Linguistics*, pages 1290–1301, Online. Association for Computational Linguistics.

Jiaao Chen and Diyi Yang. 2020. Multi-view sequence-to-sequence models with conversational structure for abstractive dialogue summarization. In *Proceedings of the 2020 Conference on Empirical Methods in Natural Language Processing (EMNLP)*, pages 4106–4118, Online. Association for Computational Linguistics.

Mingda Chen, Zewei Chu, Sam Wiseman, and Kevin Gimpel. 2022. SummScreen: A dataset for abstractive screenplay summarization. In *Proceedings of the 60th Annual Meeting of the Association for Computational Linguistics (Volume 1: Long Papers)*, pages 8602–8615, Dublin, Ireland. Association for Computational Linguistics.

Freddy Y. Y. Choi. 2000. Advances in domain independent linear text segmentation. In *1st Meeting of the North American Chapter of the Association for Computational Linguistics*.

Li Dong, Nan Yang, Wenhui Wang, Furu Wei, Xiaodong Liu, Yu Wang, Jianfeng Gao, Ming Zhou, and Hsiao-Wuen Hon. 2019. *Unified Language Model Pre-Training for Natural Language Understanding and Generation*. Curran Associates Inc., Red Hook, NY, USA.

Mike Lewis, Yinhan Liu, Naman Goyal, Marjan Ghazvininejad, Abdelrahman Mohamed, Omer Levy, Veselin Stoyanov, and Luke Zettlemoyer. 2019. BART: denoising sequence-to-sequence pre-training for natural language generation, translation, and comprehension. *CoRR*, abs/1910.13461.

Nils Reimers and Iryna Gurevych. 2019. Sentence-BERT: Sentence embeddings using Siamese BERT-networks. In *Proceedings of the 2019 Conference on Empirical Methods in Natural Language Processing and the 9th International Joint Conference on Natural Language Processing (EMNLP-IJCNLP)*, pages 3982–3992, Hong Kong, China. Association for Computational Linguistics.

Linfeng Song, Daniel Gildea, Yue Zhang, Zhiguo Wang, and Jinsong Su. 2019. Semantic neural machine translation using amr. *Transactions of the Association for Computational Linguistics*, 7:19–31.

Ashish Vaswani, Noam Shazeer, Niki Parmar, Jakob Uszkoreit, Llion Jones, Aidan N Gomez, Łukasz Kaiser, and Illia Polosukhin. 2017. Attention is All you Need. In *Advances in Neural Information Processing Systems*, volume 30. Curran Associates, Inc.

Sinong Wang, Belinda Z. Li, Madian Khabsa, Han Fang, and Hao Ma. 2020. Linformer: Self-attention with linear complexity. *CoRR*, abs/2006.04768.

Yusen Zhang, Ansong Ni, Tao Yu, Rui Zhang, Chenguang Zhu, Budhaditya Deb, Asli Celikyilmaz, Ahmed Hassan Awadallah, and Dragomir Radev. 2021. An exploratory study on long dialogue summarization: What works and what's next. In *Findings of the Association for Computational Linguistics: EMNLP 2021*, pages 4426–4433, Punta Cana, Dominican Republic. Association for Computational Linguistics.

Ming Zhong, Yang Liu, Yichong Xu, Chenguang Zhu, and Michael Zeng. 2021. Dialoglm: Pre-trained model for long dialogue understanding and summarization. *CoRR*, abs/2109.02492.

Chenguang Zhu, Ruochen Xu, Michael Zeng, and Xuedong Huang. 2020. A Hierarchical Network for Abstractive Meeting Summarization with Cross-Domain Pretraining. In *Findings of the Association for Computational Linguistics: EMNLP 2020*, pages 194–203, Online. Association for Computational Linguistics.

Jie Zhu, Junhui Li, Muhua Zhu, Longhua Qian, Min Zhang, and Guodong Zhou. 2019. Modeling graph structure in transformer for better AMR-to-text generation. In *Proceedings of the 2019 Conference on Empirical Methods in Natural Language Processing and the 9th International Joint Conference on Natural Language Processing (EMNLP-IJCNLP)*, pages 5459–5468, Hong Kong, China. Association for Computational Linguistics.

Automatic Summarization for Creative Writing: Denoising Auto-Encoder based Pipeline Method for Generating Summary of Movie Scripts

Aditya Upadhyay[&], **Nidhir Bhavsar**[$], **Aakash Bhatnagar**[1] **Muskaan Singh**[#] and **Petr Motlicek**[#]
[&] CSED, Thapar Institute of Engineering and Technology, India
[1] Boston University, Boston, Massachusetts
[$] University of Potsdam, Potsdam, Germany
[#] Speech and Audio Processing Group, IDIAP Research Institute, Martigny, Switzerland
adityaupadhyay1912@gmail.com, aakash07@bu.edu,
bhavsar@uni-potsdam.de, (msingh,petr.motlicek)@idiap.ch

Abstract

This paper documents our approach for the Creative-Summ 2022 shared task for Automatic Summarization of Creative Writing. For this purpose, we develop an automatic summarization pipeline where we leverage a denoising autoencoder for pretraining sequence-to-sequence models and fine-tune it on a large-scale abstractive screenplay summarization dataset to summarize TV transcripts from primetime shows. Our pipeline divides the input transcript into smaller conversational blocks, removes redundant text, summarises the conversational blocks, obtains the block-wise summaries, cleans, structures, and then integrates the summaries to create the meeting minutes. Our proposed system achieves first position with some of the best scores across multiple metrics (lexical, semantical) in the Creative-Summ shared task. We publicly release our proposed system here[1]

1 Introduction

Text summarization captures salient information by condensing long documents into short paragraphs. With the surge of online records, automatic text summarization makes it convenient for people to extract relevant information to their interests. There are several challenges with the current state-of-art summarization methods (i) processing long sequences spanning hundreds of pages of text, (ii) analyzing complex discourse structures such as narrative and multi-party dialogs (iii) interpreting figurative languages to understand and convey the salient points in the input. Most current works focus on the news, text, and scientific domain with limited input length, literal and technical language, hallucinations, positional biases, and constrained discourse structure. One under-explored text summarization domain is creative writing, which includes documents such as books, stories, scripts from plays, TV shows, and movies. The task of automatically summarizing the creative content is not straight forward. It involves, long length document, non-trival temporal dependency (parallel plot threads and non-linear plot development), complex structures with frequent context drifts combining narative creations and multi-party dialogs with variety of styles. In this paper we summarize these creative content of movie scripts with literary interpretations, conveying implicit information and heavily paraphrasing the input using state-of-art text summarization models.

2 Related Work

Text summarization has been a topic of research since the mid 20th century. Most earlier methods relied on statistical analysis to score the importance of sentences and then extracting the sentences with the most importance. Christian et al. (2016) proposed using TF-IDF (Term Frequency-Inverse Document Frequency) to score sentences. They found TF-IDF to be effective at extractive summarization and found it to outperform other state-of-art system available. Nomoto (2005) proposed bayesian modeling as an approach to summarize text data. Kamal proposed using extractive key concept summarization and found it to match the performance and even outperform some of the existing models at the time. Qiang et al. (2016) proposed a novel pattern based summarization technique and found it to perform much better than standard text based methods.

Following statistical methods, deep learning methods were utilized to attempt to find a solution to the problem of text summarization. Rush et al.

[1]https://github.com/aditya-u/Script-Summarization

Proceedings of the 58th Annual Meeting of the Association for Computational Linguistics, pages 44–50
July 5–10, 2020. ©2020 Association for Computational Linguistics
https://doi.org/10.26615/978-954-452-056-4_007

(2015) proposed a novel sequence-to-sequence (seq2seq) model to perform abstractive summarization rather than extractive summarization. Tan et al. (2017) proposed a novel graph based attention mechanism in a hierarchical encoder-decoder framework, and propose a hierarchical beam search algorithm to generate multi-sentence summary. This architecture provided significant improvements over previously existing models. Jiang et al. (2018) introduced a feature enhanced seq2seq model. This model improved the encode and decoder performance using a 2-feature capture network which improves the models capability of storing long term features, this makes the generated summaries far more concise and accurate.

Following the introduction of the transformer model by Vaswani et al. (2017) most work in NLP shifted to models based on the transformer architecture. Zhang et al. (2019) proposed the PEGASUS (Pre-training with Extracted Gap-sentences for Abstractive Summarization) model which demonstrated the effects of the pre-training corpora, gap-sentences ratios, vocabulary sizes and scaled up the best configuration to achieve state-of-the-art results on 12 diverse downstream datasets considered. Radford and Narasimhan (2018) introduced GPT unidirectional transformer encoder model, which improved the score of downstream NLP tasks by combining pre-training and fine tuning. Then, based on the two pre-training models, there are many fusion algorithm models to deal with the NLP task of automatic summarization. Song et al. (2019) introduced the novel MASS model, which allows the encoder and decoder to learn at the same time in the pre-training stage. It is the first time to realize the unification of the BERT plus generation model, and the rouge score is improved compared with the BERT and other models.

3 Proposed Methodology

As shown in figure 1, our suggested system is divided into three main modules, which include pre-processing input transcripts, a conventional sequence-to-sequence model for generating summaries, and post-processing, which further unifies summaries and eliminates redundant information.

3.1 Pre-Processing

The current summarization models lacks the ability to automatically ignore redundancies from a protracted dialogues. Additionally, for the models to produce accurate and high-quality text, the input must not exceed a token-length limit of $\{512, 1024\}$ tokens. This is why these models have trouble comprehending a longer string of multi-speaker utterances and the jumbled information that goes along with it. We employ an initial text processing procedure for utterance cleaning and redundancy elimination using some pre-engineered rules.

As described under the *pre-processing* section of figure 1, a raw transcript with Speaker-Utterance pairs of $X = \{(p_1, U_1), (p_2, U_2), ..., (p_L, U_L)\}$, where $p_i \subset P, 1 \geq i \geq L$ represents a participant and $U_i = \{w_1^i, w_2^i, ..., w_m^i\}$ denotes the ith utterance in a tokenized format. As said earlier, we generate a cleaned sequence, $U_i^c = \{W_1^i, W_2^i, ..., W_m^i\}$, we do this by removing unnecessary words, non UTF-8 decoded words, narration statements. To make the input utterance more redundant and reliable to be processed by the summarization model, we develope a repository of stopwords $S = \{s_1, s_2, ..., s_l\}$, which is an extension of the nltk-stopwords[2] list. We develop this by appending carefully curated vocalsound and non-regular word expression like hmm, uhm, hellooo, byeee etc. Following this, we obtain a compressed utterance, $U^{'} = U^c \cap S$

Next, Here, we use a brute-force method by breaking up the transcripts into blocks of segments with a preset token length. We do this to overcome the length restrictions of the current sequence-to-sequence summarization models. Our purpose is to retain the quality of the generated minutes while including all pertinent information in the transcripts, since we did want to be bound by the length constraint posed by the summarization model. We adopt of fluctuating set of threshold for each input-segement which might vary from $\{512, 768, 1024\}$.

3.2 Summarization

We use a finetuned BART-large model (Lewis et al., 2019) [3] for our primary summarization task. BART is a denoising autoencoder for pretraining sequence-to-sequence models. The model is trained by using arbitrary denoising functions to distort text and then instructing it to recreate the original content. Using BART provides the ability to use bi-directional attributes when operating on

[2]https://www.nltk.org/

[3]https://huggingface.co/lidiya/bart-large-xsum-samsum

sequence generation tasks which makes it useful for abstractive text summarization. While BERT cannot adopt a bidirectional mechanism for sequence generation, BART exploits the GPT-2 architecture for predicting the following words with the help of words encountered previously in the current sequence. Hence, we primarily test the pipeline with various BART-based setups. However, we majorly experiment with a fine-tuned version of BART initially trained on XSum (Narayan et al., 2018) & SAMSum (Gliwa et al., 2019) datasets. Finally, we extend the functionality of the model in sync with the proposed task by further finetuning the same using the publicly available SumScreen (Chen et al., 2021) abstractive screenplay summarization dataset.

The input sequence obtained from previous step is passed to the summarization module. For the kth segment, constituting of role-utterance pairs $X^k = \{(p_1^k, U_1^k), (p_2^k, U_2^k), ..., (p_{L_k}^k, U_{L_k}^k)\}$, the model generates a summary $C^k = \{c_1^k, c_2^k, ..., c_{L'_k}^k\}$ where c_i^k is the ith summary line of the k-th segment. Later we join all the generated summary segments to get raw aggregated summary text $Y^S = (C^1, C^2, ...C^K)$.

3.3 Post-Processing

The generated summaries contain a sufficient amount of information, although they are not entirely adequate. There might be an inclusion of casual discussion or other unnecessary information. This problem is addressed with TextRank. Based on our experimentations, we found out that from the whole report, the model typically catches 15% of trivial and unnecessary information. We rank the summary lines in increasing order of their importance and exclude out bottom 15% of the lines to obtain a "gold span" of the summary. To further compress the summaries, we add appropriate pronouns, eliminate grammatical inconsistencies wherever possible, and filter the final chain of conversation threads by excluding unnecessary words using stopwords set that we internally develop by observing the generated summaries.

4 Experimental setup

In this section, we describe dataset details in subsection 4.1, hyper-parameter setting in section 4.2 and evaluation strategy in section 4.3.

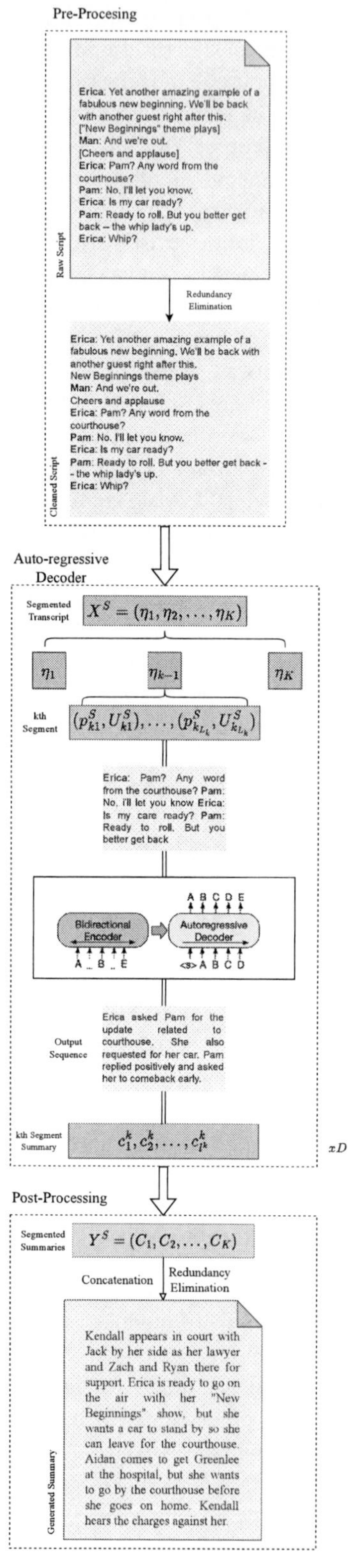

Figure 1: Proposed Architecture for BART

	value
number of shows	10
number of episodes	22503
min. episodes per show	168
max. episodes per show	3784
median episodes per show	1973.5
avg. episodes per show	2250.0

Table 1: Shows the general statistics of the SummScreen Dataset.

TV Transcript
Erica: Yet another amazing example of a fabulous new beginning. We'll be back with another guest right after this.
"New Beginnings" theme plays
Man: And we're out.
Cheers and applause
Erica: Pam? Any word from the courthouse?
Pam: No. I'll let you know.
Erica: Is my car ready?
Pam: Ready to roll. But you better get back – the whip lady's up.
Erica: Whip?
Pam: W-H-I-P? "We Help Women In Prison"? Remember?
Erica: Women in prison, Pam? With my daughter facing what she's facing? Cancel her.
Pam: The guest? She's already in the chair.
Erica: All right, all right, I will do that. But the minute I get word. I'm out of here. Thanks. Hello. Hi, nice to meet you.
SCENE_BREAK
Tad: Stop staring, Krystal.
Krystal: I'm not staring.
Tad: Yeah, you are – you're staring. Why don't you watch your daughter drool strained peaches for a while?
Krystal: Oh. Hey. Hey there. Somebody needs to talk to you about your table manners, little one. Now you're staring.
Tad: No, I'm not. It's more of a subtle glance.
Krystal: "Subtle"? Tad: Yeah. Krystal: Subtle, my eye. Come on, do we have to go?

Summary
Kendall appears in court with Jack by her side as her lawyer and Zach and Ryan there for support. Erica is ready to go on the air with her "New Beginnings" show, but she wants a car to stand by so she can leave for the courthouse. Aidan comes to get Greenlee at the hospital, but she wants to go by the courthouse before she goes on home. Kendall hears the charges against her. Kendall pleads guilty to all the charges. Kendall tells the judge everything that had led up to her stealing the chloroform from the hospital, and reporting to the police that Greenlee had stolen her little boy. Richie puts his plan in motion to place all the blame on Annie for stabbing him. Richie cons one of his inmates to pose as a doctor and call Annie to come to the hospital because his time is near. Adam and J.R. have breakfast together. Adam tries to con J.R. into moving back in with him at the tune of fifty million dollars. Krystal and Tad can't seem to keep their eyes off of Adam and J.R. Aidan and Greenlee appear in court. Greenlee asks to make a statement on Kendall's behalf. After Greenlee makes her statement, the judge calls for a recess. The judge agrees to put Kendall on probation for five years, pay fifteen thousand dollars and five hundred hours of community service. Hannah walks in just as the hearing is coming to a close. She hurries out before anyone can see her.

Figure 2: Illustrates an example derived directly from the SummScreen dataset. The first block contains the TV transcript followed by the associated summary.

4.1 Dataset

As stated, our summarization module utilizes a BART model that is initially fine-tuned on both XSum and SAMSum datasets. XSum dataset includes short summaries of articles and discussions, whereas SAMSum is a multi-party meeting conversation dataset usually comprising casual and friendly conversations. Training model on these two datasets allows it to grasp information both at the syntactic and morphological levels.

Next, to extend the model's summarization adaptability towards automatic summarization of creative writing we further train it on the SummScreen dataset. Table 1 shows the basic statistics of the SummScreen dataset. It comprises of TV transcripts and human-written recaps from primetime shows. The dataset is curated from two distinct data sources, i) TV MegaSite, Inc. (TMS) and ii) ForeverDreaming (FD). While the FD curated data contains more shows (88), spreading across 21 different genres, we train our proposed system using the TMS curated data, which includes data spanning across 4 genres with comparitavely lesser no. of shows. This is due to the fact that the FD curated data lacks original human-written recaps.

It contains 22503 transcripts taken from from TV series and their corresponding recap. The transcripts consist of dialogue utterances with speaker names, and descriptions of scenes or character actions. The recaps are human-written summaries of the corresponding transcripts. An example of snippet from the script is shown in figure 2.

4.2 Hyper-parameter Settings

For both training and inference we utilised the NVIDIA P100 GPU with 16 GB of primary memory and a hyper-threaded Intel Xeon processor with 2 cores operating at 2.3 GHz along with 52 GB of RAM. We train our summarization model for 3 Epochs with a train & evaluation batch-size of 4. During training we initialize the learning rate as 2×10^{-5} and set the max input length = 512, min target length = 128. we implement the AdaFactor optimizer, which internally adjusts the learning rate based on the scale parameter and relative/warmup steps.

4.3 Evaluation

The fine tuned and trained model was used to generate summaries for the test set provided for the shared task. This set was a previously unrevealed subset of the SummScreen test set. It contained scripts of various day time soap opera episodes. The summaries for these were generated and submitted to the shared task. They were compared to summaries of the episodes using various standard evaluation metrics such as stanza library to tokenize the summaries and then the summ_eval library to calculate ROUGE (Lin, 2004) its variants, pretrained metric such as BERTScore (Zhang et al., 2020) [4] , LitePyramid(Zhang and Bansal, 2021)

[4] microsoft/deberta-xlarge-mnli_L40_no-idf_version=0.3.9(hug_trans=4.20.1)

	A	B	C	D	E	F	G	H	I	J	K	L	M	N	O	P
Our Subm.	0.3921	0.0909	0.3794	0.5507	0.5550	0.5516	0.0740	0.0406	0.0625	0.0367	0.1133	316	1.9436	0.7618	0.2026	0.6688
Avg	0.1424	0.0222	0.1335	0.4426	0.4357	0.4354	0.0289	0.0059	0.0266	0.0044	0.0760	752	0.9139	0.6211	0.3943	0.8479

Table 2: It presents various scores obtained by our proposed summarization system on the SummScreen test dataset for the Creative-Summ 2022 automatic summarization for creative writing. It also compares our performance with average submission for the specific task. here (A)R-1 (B)R-2 (C)R-L (D)BERTScore-P (E)BERTScore-R (F)BERTScore-F1 (G)LitePyramid-p2c (H)LitePyramid-l2c (I)LitePyramid-p3c (J)LitePyramid-l3c (K)SummaCZS (L)Length (M)Density (N) Coverage (O)Novel 1-gram (P) Novel 2-grams

uses the NLI model[5], SummaCZS(Laban et al., 2022), zero-shot SummaC model on sentence-level granularity using the vitc NLI model, length of the model summaries, extractive density and coverage as (Grusky et al., 2018) and novel unigrams found in the model summaries w.r.t. the input. We have discussed our proposed system approach evaluation results further in section 5.

5 Results and Analysis

Our summarization model is evaluated on 16 unique metrics. These metrics tries to access model's performance both lexically and semantically against the human annotated summaries. Table **??** shows the evaluation results obtained on the test dataset provided under the CreativeSumm 2022 task. The test data comprises of 679 different scripts/transcripts extracted from various discrete episodes from SummScreen TMS dataset. As depicted in the table our system performs better overall in comparisons to other submission. We outperfrom their second best performing system by a margin of 0.05 across metrics like ROUGE-N, LitePyramid and SummaCZS. Our results are more adequate and fluent when referred against the original human generated annotations.

Figure 3 illustrates an actual example extracted from the SummScreen TMS dataset. It also portrays the outputs generated by passing the TV Transcripts via our proposed summarization pipeline. As it is clearly depicted our proposed system is able to extract and relate small details in the TV transcripts. These generated summaries are also grammatically tuned and adequate.

As described earlier we adopt a segmentation procedure to avoid the max-token-length conflicts posed by the current summarization models. However, a major drawback of this is that there is a loss of information which get ignored when we segement the input data. This can be solved by adopting an appropriate co-reference resolution procedure to seamlessly connect various integrative parts of the text such as noun-pronoun pairs verbs, associating adverbs which sometime due to segmentation gets disentangled. Even though, during pre-processing we try to precisely segment the text by using a floating max_threshold ranging between $\{512, 1024\}$, however sometimes these references get lost in during processing and thus might not be reflected precisely into the output text.

6 Conclusion

In this paper, we propose a unique architecture comprising of various segement working together seamlessly to produce good quality summaries of TV transcripts. We utilise a BART model initially fine-tuned on human text conversations and then on scripts specifically derived from the SummScreen TMS dataset. Our system submissions outperformed every other contribution across various evaluation metrics under the CreativeSumm 2022 task. However, the proposed pipeline still need some refinement in terms of the Language model and the inclusion of various pre-processing techniques. This could result in a significant improvement in the model's generation quality, making it more reliable and adequate.

7 Acknowledgements

This work was supported by the European Union's Horizon 2020 research and innovation program under grant agreement No. 833635 (project ROXANNE: Real-time network, text, and speaker analytics for combating organized crime, 2019-2022).

References

Mingda Chen, Zewei Chu, Sam Wiseman, and Kevin Gimpel. 2021. Summscreen: A dataset for abstractive screenplay summarization. *CoRR*, abs/2104.07091.

Hans Christian, Mikhael Agus, and Derwin Suhartono. 2016. Single document automatic text summarization using term frequency-inverse document fre-

[5] `shiyue/roberta-large-tac08`

quency (tf-idf). *ComTech: Computer, Mathematics and Engineering Applications*, 7:285.

Bogdan Gliwa, Iwona Mochol, Maciej Biesek, and Aleksander Wawer. 2019. Samsum corpus: A human-annotated dialogue dataset for abstractive summarization. *CoRR*, abs/1911.12237.

Max Grusky, Mor Naaman, and Yoav Artzi. 2018. Newsroom: A dataset of 1.3 million summaries with diverse extractive strategies. In *Proceedings of the 2018 Conference of the North American Chapter of the Association for Computational Linguistics: Human Language Technologies, NAACL-HLT 2018, New Orleans, Louisiana, USA, June 1-6, 2018, Volume 1 (Long Papers)*, pages 708–719. Association for Computational Linguistics.

Xiaoping Jiang, Po Hu, Liwei Hou, and Xia Wang. 2018. Improving pointer-generator network with keywords information for chinese abstractive summarization. In *NLPCC*.

Sarkar Kamal. Automatic single document text summarization using key concepts in documents automatic single document text summarization using key concepts in documents. *Journal of Information Processing Systems* , 9(4):602–620.

Philippe Laban, Tobias Schnabel, Paul N. Bennett, and Marti A. Hearst. 2022. Summac: Re-visiting nli-based models for inconsistency detection in summarization. *Trans. Assoc. Comput. Linguistics*, 10:163–177.

Mike Lewis, Yinhan Liu, Naman Goyal, Marjan Ghazvininejad, Abdelrahman Mohamed, Omer Levy, Veselin Stoyanov, and Luke Zettlemoyer. 2019. BART: denoising sequence-to-sequence pre-training for natural language generation, translation, and comprehension. *CoRR*, abs/1910.13461.

Chin-Yew Lin. 2004. Rouge: A package for automatic evaluation of summaries. In *Text summarization branches out*, pages 74–81.

Shashi Narayan, Shay B. Cohen, and Mirella Lapata. 2018. Don't give me the details, just the summary! topic-aware convolutional neural networks for extreme summarization. *CoRR*, abs/1808.08745.

Tadashi Nomoto. 2005. Bayesian learning in text summarization. In *Proceedings of Human Language Technology Conference and Conference on Empirical Methods in Natural Language Processing*, pages 249–256, Vancouver, British Columbia, Canada. Association for Computational Linguistics.

Ji-Peng Qiang, Ping Chen, Wei Ding, Fei Xie, and Xindong Wu. 2016. Multi-document summarization using closed patterns. *Knowledge-Based Systems*, 99:28–38.

Alec Radford and Karthik Narasimhan. 2018. Improving language understanding by generative pre-training.

Alexander M. Rush, Sumit Chopra, and Jason Weston. 2015. A neural attention model for abstractive sentence summarization. In *Proceedings of the 2015 Conference on Empirical Methods in Natural Language Processing*, pages 379–389, Lisbon, Portugal. Association for Computational Linguistics.

Kaitao Song, Xu Tan, Tao Qin, Jianfeng Lu, and Tie-Yan Liu. 2019. Mass: Masked sequence to sequence pre-training for language generation.

Jiwei Tan, Xiaojun Wan, and Jianguo Xiao. 2017. Abstractive document summarization with a graph-based attentional neural model. In *Proceedings of the 55th Annual Meeting of the Association for Computational Linguistics (Volume 1: Long Papers)*, pages 1171–1181, Vancouver, Canada. Association for Computational Linguistics.

Ashish Vaswani, Noam Shazeer, Niki Parmar, Jakob Uszkoreit, Llion Jones, Aidan N. Gomez, Lukasz Kaiser, and Illia Polosukhin. 2017. Attention is all you need.

Jingqing Zhang, Yao Zhao, Mohammad Saleh, and Peter J. Liu. 2019. Pegasus: Pre-training with extracted gap-sentences for abstractive summarization.

Shiyue Zhang and Mohit Bansal. 2021. Finding a balanced degree of automation for summary evaluation. In *Proceedings of the 2021 Conference on Empirical Methods in Natural Language Processing, EMNLP 2021, Virtual Event / Punta Cana, Dominican Republic, 7-11 November, 2021*, pages 6617–6632. Association for Computational Linguistics.

Tianyi Zhang, Varsha Kishore, Felix Wu, Kilian Q. Weinberger, and Yoav Artzi. 2020. Bertscore: Evaluating text generation with BERT. In *8th International Conference on Learning Representations, ICLR 2020, Addis Ababa, Ethiopia, April 26-30, 2020*. OpenReview.net.

A Appendix

TV Transcript
Knock on door J.R.: Hey. Babe: Hey. J.R.: Can I come in? Since Im̃ no longer a suspected criminal, I figured we could do a more personal Christmas a little later on. Babe: Yeah. Yeah, come on in. J.R.: All right. Babe: So, what happened, J.R.? I mean, did you finally remember where you were the night Zach was hit? J.R.: With a little help from my mom. Itś a long story. Babe: So – J.R.: Well, a gentlemanś not supposed to kiss and tell, but I guess it depends on who the lady is. I was with Amanda, I was drunk as a skunk, and I told her every rotten thing that Iv́e ever done. Babe: And she never said anything? J.R.: Payback is sweet. Babe: That bitch! J.R.: Im̃ not going to argue with you on that one. But you want to know what the best part is? The cherry on top of the Christmas pie? Guess who else knew the truth and buried it like a bone in the backyard? Babe: Youŕe kidding. J.R.: Nope. Thanks again, Dad, for everything. SCENE BREAK Adam: Hello, Stuart, itś your brother. ...
Human Recaps
Adam calls Stuart and tries to set up a time for them to have coffee together. Hannah comes in with a folder in her hand and tells Adam that she had what he wanted, Zach's head on a platter. Jack visits Greenlee and inquires if she trusts him. J.R. visits Babe, bearing gifts. He lets her know what had happened and how Amanda had set him up, and that Adam had known about it all along. Kendall is brought into an interrogation room. Zach walks up to the door and asks her why is she throwing everything away. Jack comes into the room and tells Kendall that he would like to represent her. Aidan visits Greenlee. Greenlee tells him that she thinks everyone had done a 180. Aidan was friends with Kendall and Greenlee was friends with Zach. Greenlee can't understand why Kendall is doing this. Hannah fills Adam in on what she had done to Zach and how everything now belongs to Adam. In putting the presents under the tree, J.R. finds one to Richie from Babe. Richie's doc from the prison visits him. Richie lets him know that he has chosen the day in which he is going to die, but he is leaving the insurance money to Babe instead of him
Generated Summary
J.R. was with Amanda the night Zach was hit. J.R was drunk and told Amanda everything he did wrong. Jack wants to clear his conscience by telling the truth about Greenlee and Kendall. Jack is doing it for Greenlee's sake. Kendall is turning herself in to the police. Hannah sold Chandler Enterprises in pieces to Adam. Adam will buy it back cheaper. Jack will prepare a strategy to knock some of the charges against her down. Kendall doesn't want to go to jail, but she's not going to take responsibility for all of that. Richie has changed the beneficiary of his insurance policy. Richie is going to die next week. Hannah took a job at Chandler Enterprises, but she doesn't want to work anymore. Adam offers her to be her concubine. Adam and Hannah argue. Adam thinks Hannah's talents are considerable, but he wouldn't overrate them. Hannah took the job because she was threatened by Alexander Cambias and she still loves Zach Slater. Kendall is in prison. Zach is angry at him because he broke his promise to God and to his family. Joe wants to have some additional blood work done on Greenlee Smythe. Little Adam drew Daddy a picture. Winnie helped Little Adam with it. Kendall and Zach kiss passionately. Annie and Richie are about to die. Adam and J.R. want to be father and son again. Kendall won't lie to the judge.

Figure 3: Illustrates an actual example derived from the SummScreen TMS dataset along with the output generated using our proposed summarization system.

The CreativeSumm 2022 Shared Task: A Two-Stage Summarization Model using Scene Attributes

EunChong Kim* **TaeWoo Yoo*** **GunHee Cho** **SuYoung Bae** **Yun-Gyung Cheong**
Department of Artificial Intelligence
Sungkyunkwan University, South Korea
{prokkec,woo990307,skate4333,sybae01,aimecca}@skku.edu

Abstract

In this paper, we describe our work for the CreativeSumm 2022 Shared Task, Automatic Summarization for Creative Writing. The task is to summarize movie scripts, which is challenging due to their long length and complex format. To tackle this problem, we present a two-stage summarization approach using both the abstractive and an extractive summarization methods. In addition, we preprocess the script to enhance summarization performance. The results of our experiment demonstrate that the presented approach outperforms baseline models in terms of standard summarization evaluation metrics.

1 Introduction

Summarization is an important task in natural language processing research area. Although many works have been conducted on summarization, little has been researched on summarizing movie scripts. It is challenging to generate a summary from movie scripts for several reasons. First, movie scripts are long. According to an analysis on Hollywood screenplays Snyder (2005), a typical script has an average page count of 110, and can even reach a few hundred pages. The long input length causes disparities when aligning its plot summary with corresponding parts in the script (Mirza et al., 2021).

Summarizing long and multi-faceted document is a classical challenge. As the document gets longer, the computational complexity of summarizing it increases dramatically (Gidiotis and Tsoumakas, 2020). Attempts have been made to address the problem of long document summarization, utilizing discourse in the document (Cohan et al., 2018) and hierarchical structures to effectively understand long sentences (Grail et al., 2021). Cohan et al. (2018) recognizes the importance of discourse in long document summarization. They develop a discourse-aware decoder to capture important points from different discourse sections. Liu et al. (2018) presents a two-stage strategy. They select important sentences in a document using an extractive summarization model, and then summarize them again using a transformer decoder.

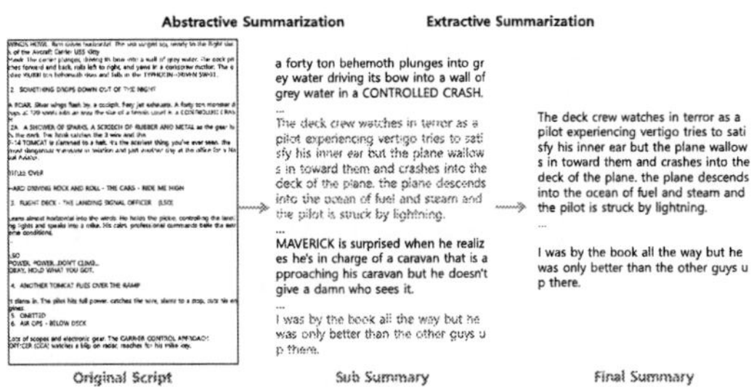

Figure 1: A sample illustration of our two-stage summarization approach with the movie script of the film 'Top Gun'. We first create a scene summary from the script using an abstractive summarization model. We then select important sentences using an extractive summarization model.

Moreover, movie scripts have a complex format, consisting of different components such as dialogues, action directions, scene description, cut transitions, film editing instructions, etc (Feng et al., 2021). Movie transcripts are similar to TV scripts, in that they contain dialogues as well as action and filming directions and editing descriptions. Various studies have been conducted to extract summaries from TV scripts (Liu et al., 2021). Zhong et al. (2022) constructs a dialogue summarization model trained with TV transcripts datasets by crawling them from the websites such as Forever Dreaming and TVMegaSite dataset (Chen et al., 2021a). Although movie scripts tend to be longer than TV scripts, we can refer to previous studies in TV script summarization to deal with the complex format.

Summarization methods can be divided into two types: abstractive and extractive summarization. When a document is given as a source text, an abstractive summarization generates a summary that

Proceedings of the 58th Annual Meeting of the Association for Computational Linguistics, pages 51–56
July 5–10, 2020. ©2020 Association for Computational Linguistics
https://doi.org/10.26615/978-954-452-056-4_008

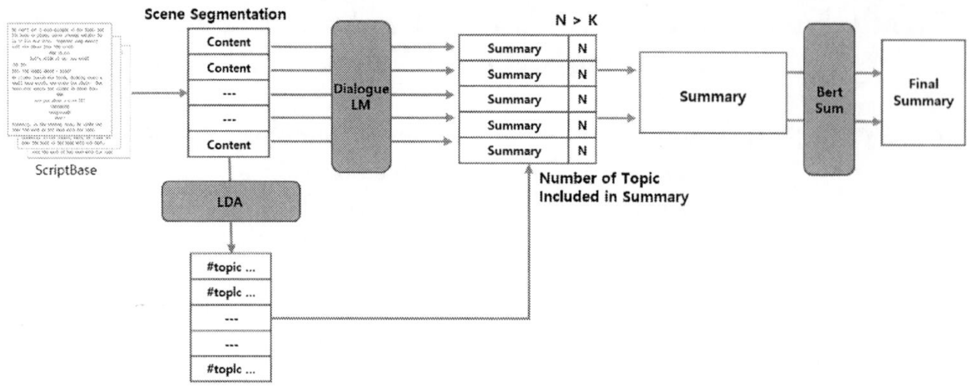

Figure 2: Framework of our model contains scene segmentation, abstractive summarization using Dialogue LM, important scene selection, and extractive summarization using BERTSum.

contains text that are not in the source text, whereas extractive summarization re-uses the words in the source text. Specifically, the task of extractive summarization is choosing salient words and sentences.

The goal of our work is to summarize movie scripts, which is one of the shared task of CreativeSumm 2022, the Automatic Summarization for Creative Writing workshop, at COLING 2022. This paper describes a two-stage summarization approach employing both the abstractive and extractive summarization methods to summarize movie scripts.

Figure 1 illustrates our framework. First, our preprocessing stage merges similar scenes based on character information to enhance the summarization performance. Then, the abstractive summarization method produces a summary for each scene-based unit of the script. In particular, we use the DialogLM model (Zhong et al., 2022) since dialogues in the script are essential for understanding the story. Finally, these scene summaries are summarized again by selecting salient scenes via topic modeling and the extractive summarization method.

This paper is structured as follows. Section 2 describes our method in detail. Section 3 reports the results of the experiment. Finally, we end with conclusion.

2 Method

Our approach is composed of four steps: scene segmentation, dialogue abstraction, salient scene selection, and extractive summarization. Figure 2 briefly illustrate our method.

2.1 Scene Segmentation

Before putting the script into the abstract summarization model, we preprocess the script to group scenes with similar context. Generally, one sentence of a plot summary can be mapped to several scenes in the script (Mirza et al., 2021). Hence, we first divide the script into scenes, using scene headings that describe the location and time of the day of a scene, such as 'INT', 'EXT', '-DAY', and '-NIGHT', following (Mirza et al., 2021).

Then, we group a number of scene based on the main characters, as illustrated in Figure 3. First, we identify main characters based on the number of scenes they appear. For this, we set the total number of scenes as the threshold value. In the example, the script contains 100 scenes which serves as the threshold. We count the number of scenes that a character appears. Starting from the highest value, we accumulate the numbers of character appearance until their sum exceeds the threshold. As a result, Woody, Buzz, and Andy are identified as the main characters. We classify the characters contributing to the summation as main characters. Therefore, the main characters in our approach can be different from the actual main characters in the movie.

Then, we merge subsequent scenes where their main characters are identical. For instance, scenes 10 and 11 are merged since they share Woody and Buzz as the main characters, however, scenes 11 and 12 are not merged since Woody is not present in scene 12.

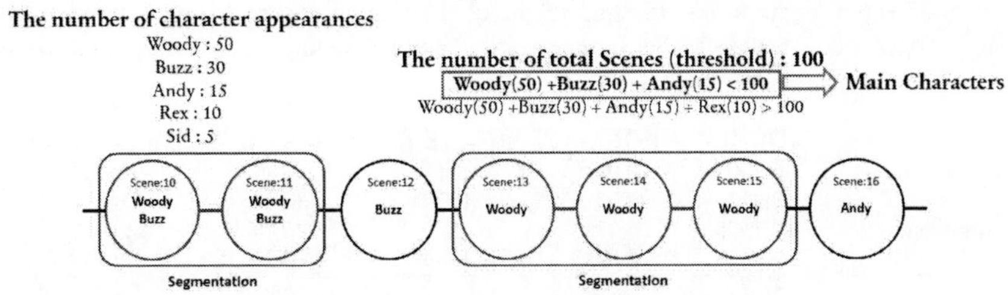

Figure 3: An example of scene merging process. The first step identifies main characters. The second step merges the consecutive scenes into one if their main characters are identical.

Movie_name	Content	Scene_number	Scene_summary	Topic_list	Include_topic_num
Movie38	In a paneled room tastefully hung with a few	[4]	Klingman becomes an arbitrageur when he convin...	['wash','know','brand y','look,''speak'......]	8
Movie38	The rubber-gloved hands are gluing the sord	[5,6,7,8,9]	The film is set in a rural stucco home of a ma....	['look','read', 'doll', 'open', 'note', 'piece' ......]	10
Movie38	Frank lounges in his shorts under the single	[10,11]	Frank's knifethrowing is thwarted by	['throw','post','knives' ,'knife',stand' ......]	9

Figure 4: An example of important scene selection using topic modeling. We compute the scene's salience score as the number of keywords that are associated with the scene's main topic. In this case, the summary of the scenes [5,6,7,8] scores highest.

2.2 Dialogue Abstraction

This step uses an abstractive summarization model to summarize a scene. In a script, a scene has dialogues between characters mixed with various information such as action direction and film editing instructions. Since dialogues are essential for story comprehension, we believe dialogue summarization models are appropriate for abstracting a scene.

Various studies have been conducted on dialogue summarization tasks (Gliwa et al., 2019; Chen et al., 2021b; Feng et al., 2022): a study on dialogue summarization using a graph with topic words (Zhao et al., 2020), a study using a model with sparse attention technology and pre-training with a new masking skill to improve dialogue summarization performance (Zhong et al., 2022), etc.

In this study, we apply the abstractive summarization model DialogLM (Zhong et al., 2022) to each scene to generate a scene summary. We did not eliminate other supplemental components such as film editing instructions and action descriptions. In our work, we observe that a scene summary typically consists of 80 tokens, while the maximum length of a summary is set to 280 tokens.

2.3 Important Scene Selection

The previous step creates scene summaries. Since not all the scenes contribute equally to story comprehension, we select important scenes using a topic modeling approach. We leverage LDA to find topics that are associated with a particular scene summary where individual topic is also associated with $N(=10$ in our work) topic. Latent Dirichlet Allocation (LDA) (Blei et al., 2003) is a probabilistic topic modeling method that infers latent topics from a corpus of documents.

We select a single keyword from each scene summary with the highest proportion as its main topic. For example, if a scene summary is associated with three topics, such that topic 1 occupies 74%, topic 2 occupies 20%, and topic 3 occupies 6% of the summary, we select topic 1 as the main topic of that scene. We compute the salience score of the scene summary based on the number of keywords that are associated with the scene's main topic (see Figure 4). If these keywords appear in a scene summary less than the pre-defined threshold value, we eliminate the summary from the scene summaries set.

Table 1: Results of experiments to test the impact of scene merging and replacing extractive summary with abstractive summary. AS denotes abstracive summarization, and ES denotes extractive summarization. The best performance is shown in bold.

	ROUGE-1	ROUGE-2	ROUGE-L	BERTScore-P	BERTScore-R	BERTScore-F1
AS + AS (w.o scene merge)	0.3003	0.0490	0.1311	0.6185	0.6611	0.6385
AS + AS	0.3226	0.0578	0.1375	0.6434	0.6643	0.6488
AS + ES (w.o scene merge)	0.3975	0.0788	0.1529	0.6780	0.6932	0.6854
AS + ES	**0.4010**	**0.0788**	**0.1580**	**0.6835**	**0.6953**	**0.6892**

2.4 Extractive Summarization

At this stage, only important scene summaries remain. The final step leverages an extractive summarization model to create the final summary of the film.

We use the BERTSum model(Liu, 2019), which uses BERT(Devlin et al., 2018) as the embedding model. In BERTSum, the input document is encoded with multiple sentences and then used as the input for BERT. Then, use the output of the BERT as the input to the summarization layers of the Transformer 2-layers. Finally, Using the sigmoid function to classify each sentence as class 0 or class 1. The scene summaries are given as input to BERTSum, and only the scene summaries classified as class 1 are included in the final summary.

3 Evaluation

3.1 Dataset

The goal of our work is to summarize movie scripts, which is one of the CreativeSumm 2022 shared tasks. We are provided with ScriptBase (Gorinski and Lapata, 2015), a collection of 1,276 movie scripts and their corresponding wikiplot summaries, as the training and development dataset. An additional dataset is provided as the test dataset for evaluating our approach using standard automatic evaluation metrics including ROUGE, BERTScore, LitePyramid, and SummaCZS.

3.2 Model selection

To find the best setting for our method, we conducted several experiments with various settings using 100 randomly selected movies from the dataset. First, we test whether the scene grouping method enhances the summarization performance or not. We simply remove scene segmentation process and check how this impacts the model performance. Table 1 shows that we obtained the best performance when using an extractive summarization model with the scene merging strategy.

Second, we test if the extractive summarization method can replace abstractive summarization. We use Primer (Xiao et al., 2021) as the abstractive summarization model which specializes summarizing long/multi documents. As described above, BertSum (Liu, 2019) is used as the extractive summarization model. Table 1 shows that using the abstractive model throughout the summarization process results in performance deterioration regardless of the scene merging strategy. Therefore, we use the scene merging strategy and the combination of abstractive and extractive summarizaion for the evaluation.

3.3 Model settings

We leverage DialogLM and BertSum models for abstractive and extractive summarization respectively. DialogLM, used in this experiment, is DialogLED-base-16384, a larger version of DialogLM. We fine-tune the pre-trained DialogLM model on the FD dataset (Chen et al., 2021a), which has transcripts of 88 TV shows. This model accepts up to 16,384 tokens as input and outputs a summary consisting of up to 280 tokens. We use the BertSum model that employs the Bert model pre-trained with the pytorch-pre-trained-BERT version. We constrain the summary length not to exceed 4500 tokens.

3.4 Results

Table 2 shows the evaluation metrics (ROUGE, BERTScore (Zhang et al., 2019), LitePyramid (Zhang and Bansal, 2021), and SummaC (Laban et al., 2021)) computed on the test dataset. The baseline model is LED (Beltagy et al., 2020), with variations of input size of 1024, 4096, and 16384.

The results indicate that our approach outperforms the baseline model in terms of the ROUGE and BERTScore metrics. BERTScore use BERT to calculate similarity score between candidate sentence and reference sentence in each token. We obtained 0.4144 for ROUGE-1, 0.0823 for ROUGE-2, and 0.3963 for ROUGE-3, achieving three times better results than the baseline model. Our ap-

Table 2: The evaluation metrics of the experiment on the test set. The subscript denotes input size. The best performance is shown in bold.

	ROUGE-1	ROUGE-2	ROUGE-L	BERTScore-P	BERTScore-R	BERTScore-F1
LED_{1024}	0.1492	0.0146	0.1373	0.4298	0.4238	0.4258
LED_{4096}	0.1416	0.0130	0.1299	0.4245	0.4137	0.4179
LED_{16384}	0.1368	0.0125	0.1277	0.4322	0.3924	0.4099
Our approach	**0.4144**	**0.0823**	**0.3963**	**0.5163**	**0.5233**	**0.5194**

	LitePyramid-p^{2c}	LitePyramid-l^{2c}	LitePyramid-p^{3c}	LitePyramid-l^{3c}	SummaCZS
LED_{1024}	**0.3436**	0.3546	0.2517	0.2833	0.0000
LED_{4096}	0.3604	**0.3763**	**0.2674**	**0.3042**	0.0000
LED_{16384}	0.3009	0.3082	0.2312	0.2602	0.0000
Our approach	0.0370	0.0063	0.0356	0.0072	**0.0476**

	Length	Density	Coverage	Novel 1-grams	Novel 2-grams
LED_{1024}	903	1.1809	0.7021	**0.3357**	**0.7485**
LED_{4096}	877	1.3432	0.7311	0.3092	0.7273
LED_{16384}	551	1.4103	0.7266	0.3024	0.7211
Our approach	729	**3.4398**	**0.8759**	0.1621	0.4827

proach also outperforms the baseline models in terms of the density and coverage metrics. The density score denotes the average length of the extractive fragment in the summary, and the coverage score denotes how many words in the document are included in the summary (Grusky et al., 2018). Since we use an extractive summarization model to create the final summary, the Novel n-grams scores tend to be low (see Table 2).

Our approach underperforms for various LitePyramid metrics, which compare the reference with system summary using a natural language inference (NLI) model. But we get good score at SummaCZS, which compute NLI score between pairs of sentences from segmented document. Length denotes the average length of the summaries that the model produces.

4 Conclusion

In this paper, we present a two-stage approach for the shared task of Creative-Summ 2022. We first segment the script into scenes and create their summaries using an abstractive summarization model. Second, we apply topic modeling to eliminate less important scenes. Then, a BERT-based extractive summarization model generates the final summary of the movie. The result of evaluation indicates that our approach outperforms baseline models in several metrics. We got 0.4144 for ROUGE-1, 0.0823 for ROUGE-2, and 0.3963 for ROUGE-3 which are better than baseline models. We also got better BERTScore such as 0.5163 for precision, 0.5233 for recall and 0.5194 for F1 score.

Acknowledgments

This work was partly supported by the National Research Foundation of Korea(NRF) grant funded by the Korea government(MEST) (No. 2019R1A2C1006316), Institute of Information & communications Technology Planning & Evaluation(IITP) grant funded by the Korea government(MSIT) (No.2019-0-00421, Artificial Intelligence Graduate School Program(Sungkyunkwan University)), and NCSoft.

References

Iz Beltagy, Matthew E Peters, and Arman Cohan. 2020. Longformer: The long-document transformer. *arXiv preprint arXiv:2004.05150*.

David M Blei, Andrew Y Ng, and Michael I Jordan. 2003. Latent dirichlet allocation. *Journal of machine Learning research*, 3(Jan):993–1022.

Mingda Chen, Zewei Chu, Sam Wiseman, and Kevin Gimpel. 2021a. Summscreen: A dataset for abstractive screenplay summarization. *CoRR*, abs/2104.07091.

Yulong Chen, Yang Liu, Liang Chen, and Yue Zhang. 2021b. Dialogsum: A real-life scenario dialogue summarization dataset. *arXiv preprint arXiv:2105.06762*.

Arman Cohan, Franck Dernoncourt, Doo Soon Kim, Trung Bui, Seokhwan Kim, Walter Chang, and Nazli Goharian. 2018. A discourse-aware attention model for abstractive summarization of long documents. *arXiv preprint arXiv:1804.05685*.

Jacob Devlin, Ming-Wei Chang, Kenton Lee, and Kristina Toutanova. 2018. Bert: Pre-training of deep bidirectional transformers for language understanding. *arXiv preprint arXiv:1810.04805*.

Xiachong Feng, Xiaocheng Feng, and Bing Qin. 2021. A survey on dialogue summarization: Recent advances and new frontiers. *arXiv preprint arXiv:2107.03175*.

Xiachong Feng, Xiaocheng Feng, and Bing Qin. 2022. Msamsum: Towards benchmarking multi-lingual dialogue summarization. In *Proceedings of the Second DialDoc Workshop on Document-grounded Dialogue and Conversational Question Answering*, pages 1–12.

Alexios Gidiotis and Grigorios Tsoumakas. 2020. A divide-and-conquer approach to the summarization of long documents. *IEEE/ACM Transactions on Audio, Speech, and Language Processing*, 28:3029–3040.

Bogdan Gliwa, Iwona Mochol, Maciej Biesek, and Aleksander Wawer. 2019. Samsum corpus: A human-annotated dialogue dataset for abstractive summarization. *arXiv preprint arXiv:1911.12237*.

Philip Gorinski and Mirella Lapata. 2015. Movie script summarization as graph-based scene extraction. In *Proceedings of the 2015 Conference of the North American Chapter of the Association for Computational Linguistics: Human Language Technologies*, pages 1066–1076.

Quentin Grail, Julien Perez, and Eric Gaussier. 2021. Globalizing bert-based transformer architectures for long document summarization. In *Proceedings of the 16th Conference of the European Chapter of the Association for Computational Linguistics: Main Volume*, pages 1792–1810.

Max Grusky, Mor Naaman, and Yoav Artzi. 2018. Newsroom: A dataset of 1.3 million summaries with diverse extractive strategies. *arXiv preprint arXiv:1804.11283*.

Philippe Laban, Tobias Schnabel, Paul N Bennett, and Marti A Hearst. 2021. Summac: Re-visiting nli-based models for inconsistency detection in summarization. *arXiv preprint arXiv:2111.09525*.

Junpeng Liu, Yanyan Zou, Hainan Zhang, Hongshen Chen, Zhuoye Ding, Caixia Yuan, and Xiaojie Wang. 2021. Topic-aware contrastive learning for abstractive dialogue summarization. *arXiv preprint arXiv:2109.04994*.

Peter J Liu, Mohammad Saleh, Etienne Pot, Ben Goodrich, Ryan Sepassi, Lukasz Kaiser, and Noam Shazeer. 2018. Generating wikipedia by summarizing long sequences. *arXiv preprint arXiv:1801.10198*.

Yang Liu. 2019. Fine-tune bert for extractive summarization. *arXiv preprint arXiv:1903.10318*.

Paramita Mirza, Mostafa Abouhamra, and Gerhard Weikum. 2021. Alignarr: Aligning narratives on movies. In *The 59th Annual Meeting of the Association for Computational Linguistics and the 11th International Joint Conference on Natural Language Processing*, pages 427–433. ACL.

Blake Snyder. 2005. Save the cat! the last book on screenwriting you'll ever need.

Wen Xiao, Iz Beltagy, Giuseppe Carenini, and Arman Cohan. 2021. Primer: Pyramid-based masked sentence pre-training for multi-document summarization. *arXiv preprint arXiv:2110.08499*.

Shiyue Zhang and Mohit Bansal. 2021. Finding a balanced degree of automation for summary evaluation. *arXiv preprint arXiv:2109.11503*.

Tianyi Zhang, Varsha Kishore, Felix Wu, Kilian Q Weinberger, and Yoav Artzi. 2019. Bertscore: Evaluating text generation with bert. *arXiv preprint arXiv:1904.09675*.

Lulu Zhao, Weiran Xu, and Jun Guo. 2020. Improving abstractive dialogue summarization with graph structures and topic words. In *Proceedings of the 28th International Conference on Computational Linguistics*, pages 437–449.

Ming Zhong, Yang Liu, Yichong Xu, Chenguang Zhu, and Michael Zeng. 2022. Dialoglm: Pre-trained model for long dialogue understanding and summarization. In *Proceedings of the AAAI Conference on Artificial Intelligence*, volume 36, pages 11765–11773.

Two-Stage Movie Script Summarization: An Efficient Method For Low-Resource Long Document Summarization

Dongqi Pu*, **Xudong Hong***†, **Pin-Jie Lin***, **Ernie Chang** and **Vera Demberg**
†Max Planck Institute for Informatics
Saarland University, Saarland Informatics Campus, Germany
`{dongqipu,pinjie}@lst.uni-saarland.de`
`{xhong,cychang,vera}@coli.uni-saarland.de`

Abstract

The Creative Summarization Shared Task at COLING 2022 aspires to generate summaries given long-form texts from creative writing. This paper presents the system architecture and the results of our participation in the Scriptbase track that focuses on generating movie plots given movie scripts. The core innovation in our model employs a two-stage hierarchical architecture for movie script summarization. In the first stage, a heuristic extraction method is applied to extract actions and essential dialogues, which reduces the average length of input movie scripts by 66% from about 24K to 8K tokens. In the second stage, a state-of-the-art encoder-decoder model, Longformer-Encoder-Decoder (LED), is trained with effective fine-tuning methods, *BitFit* and *NoisyTune*. Evaluations on the unseen test set indicate that our system outperforms both zero-shot LED baselines as well as other participants on various automatic metrics and ranks 1st in the Scriptbase track[1].

1 Introduction

The goal of the Creative Summarization Shared Task 2022 (`ASCW@COLING'22`) is to automatically generate summaries based on long-form creative texts like literature, movie scripts, or TV screenplays. This task is encouraged by practical settings in part by the condition to reflect the information that is realistically available in real-world natural language generation task – realistic texts like movie scripts and plot summaries can be *prohibitively long* (See *Movie Script* and *Plot Summary* in Figure 1).

Current dominant neural approaches to long document summarization (Zhang et al., 2020; Xiao et al., 2022; Guo et al., 2022) mainly embrace neural sequence-to-sequence architectures consisting of an encoder-decoder setup where the entire input sequence is first encoded before decoding the output sequence autoregressively. While the encoder-decoder architecture is triumphant in natural language generation tasks (Peng et al., 2020a; Akermi et al., 2020; Erdem et al., 2022; Qian et al., 2022), it is not without its challenges, some of which are exacerbated in this shared task.

In particular, the challenges in this shared task stem from the inherent characteristics of the corpus, which consists of not only texts (i.e. scripts of 24K tokens) that are much longer than the context length of current state-of-the-art long document summarizers (e.g. 16K in LongT5 (Guo et al., 2022)), but also requires that the decoder be exploited of its long-term attention capabilities to an extreme extent and generate up to summaries of 1K tokens. The excessively long decoding time made it impossible to experiment with different model architectures and perform extensive hyperparameter tuning for model selection. Therefore, the optimization space during training time is severely limited; and the inference step becomes highly time-consuming for experimentation during the trial and error process.

To this end, our system employs a two-stage procedure for movie script to movie plot summarization. In the first stage, we propose to heuristically extract sentences that effectively reduce the average input length from 24K to 8K tokens. Next, we propose to improve upon the Longformer-based encoder-decoder model (LED) (Beltagy et al., 2020) by coupling it with two effective fine-tuning methods, i.e., BitFit (Ben Zaken et al., 2022) where only the bias-terms (0.09% of the parameters) of the model are being updated and NoisyTune (Wu et al., 2022) where employs a matrix-level perturbation strategy to increase the variation amplitude of the parameters.

∗ These authors contributed equally to this work.

[1]Source code and pre-trained models are available at: `https://github.com/tony-hong/script-2-story`

Proceedings of the 58th Annual Meeting of the Association for Computational Linguistics, pages 57–66
July 5–10, 2020. ©2020 Association for Computational Linguistics
https://doi.org/10.26615/978-954-452-056-4_009

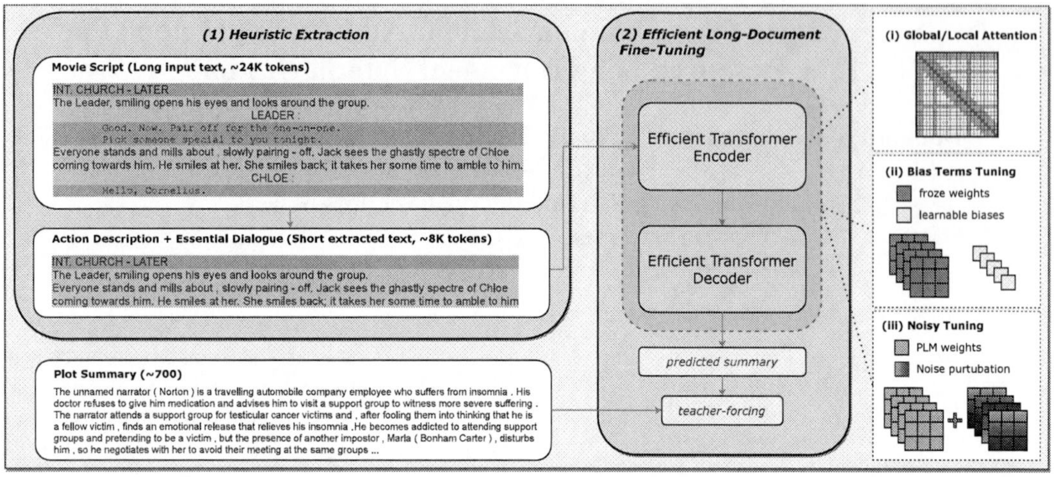

Figure 1: Diagram to depict the pipeline. Our system achieves efficient text summarization by (1) heuristics extraction method to compress long input text into a relatively short input sequence, and (2) efficient long-document fine-tuning. In the first stage, the heuristics extraction method takes (a) long movie scripts with an average length of 24K and compress them into 8K. (b) Following that, the transformer encoder with (i) global sliding winding attention takes movie scripts up to 8K tokens and is jointly fine-tuned with the decoder using (ii) bias-terms tuning or (iii) noisy tuning techniques to generate a long movie summarization (1K) in a computationally efficient manner.

Further, we start to tease apart the intricate relationship between decoding beam size, model performance, and maximum encoder and decoder lengths in our ablation studies (see Section 3.6). We examine the trade-offs between performance and decoding runtime, and empirically find that beam search size = 4 is the most suitable.

To summarize, our contributions are as follows:

1. We describe the long-form challenge in this shared task as a challenge that impacts not only the model performance but also the model training and evaluation.

2. We propose a two-stage solution to solving this challenge by first reducing its average input length, and then incorporating the Longformer architecture with either a simple yet effective finetuning technique (BitFit) or a matrix-wise perturbing method for finetuning (NoisyTune).

3. We are the first to apply the transformer-based model for summarization on this dataset (Scriptbase), and our model ranks 1st on metrics including ROUGE, BERTScore, and N-gram diversities.

2 Our Approach

Our method is a two-stage summarization method where the 1st stage is a heuristic extraction method (Sec. 2.1) and the 2nd stage is neural seq2seq summarization model (Sec. 2.2).

2.1 Heuristic Extraction Method

Because the average input length (24K) is way beyond the maximum context length of SOTA long-text summarization models, e.g., 16K in LongT5 (Guo et al., 2022). We are required to first reduce input text length by applying heuristics about what parts of the input to drop.

Specifically, for each of the movie scripts, which consist of two elements: (1) *action* (red and grey in Figure 1*(1)*), descriptions of events or expressions that can be heard by the audiences; (2) *dialogue* (green and blue in Figure 1*(1)*), conversations between characters. We first identify all the titles and texts of actions and dialogues. Then we extract the titles and texts of all actions with regular expression because they deliver essential information about the movies. However, some important concepts are only in the dialogues (Gorinski and Lapata, 2015). According to the narrative structures of movie scripts (Lee et al., 2021), when a new character occurs, the first few dialogues contain introductory concepts about this character. So our heuristics also include these essential dialogues in our input.

2.2 Long Document Encoder-Decoder

Bottleneck of Transformer Transformer-based models, based on the multi-head self-attention (MHSA) mechanism (Vaswani et al., 2017), are allowed to simultaneously attend to the con-

Dataset	R-1	R-2	R-L	BS-P	BS-R	BS-F1	S	1-G	2-G
LED-1024	13.68	1.25	12.77	43.22	39.24	40.99	0.00	30.24	72.11
LED-4096	14.16	1.30	12.99	42.45	41.37	41.79	0.00	30.92	72.73
LED-16384	14.92	1.46	13.73	42.98	42.38	42.58	0.00	33.57	74.85
MovING	41.44	8.23	39.63	51.63	52.33	51.94	**4.76**	16.21	48.27
UdS	**46.39**	11.52	**44.08**	57.03	56.72	56.86	2.69	34.56	76.04
UdS NoisyTune	46.34	**11.58**	44.05	**57.23**	**56.80**	**57.00**	2.50	**35.20**	**76.36**
UdS BitFit	45.76	**11.58**	43.80	56.90	56.20	56.53	3.01	31.67	74.59

Table 1: Results of the proposed model on unseen test set compared to other systems using automatic metrics including ROUGE-1 F1 (R-1), ROUGE-2 F1 (R-2), ROUGE-L F1 (R-L), BERTScore-Precision (BS-P), BERTScore-Recall (BS-R), BERTScore-F1 (BS-F1), SummaCZS (S), Novel 1-grams (1-G) and Novel 2-grams (2-G).

text at different positions from different representation subspaces: $\mathrm{MHSA}(\mathbf{Q}_i, \mathbf{K}_i, \mathbf{V}_i) = [\mathbf{A}_1, \mathbf{A}_2, ..., \mathbf{A}_h]\mathbf{W}^O + \mathbf{B}^O$ where $\mathbf{Q}_i, \mathbf{K}_i, \mathbf{V}_i \in \mathbb{R}^{t\times d}$ are the input attention matrices, t is the sequence length, d_m is the model embedding dimension, $\mathbf{A}_i$ is the i-th attention head, h is the number of attention heads, and $\mathbf{W}^O \in \mathbb{R}^{d_m\times d_m}$ is the parameter matrix and $\mathbf{B}^O \in \mathbb{R}^{t\times d_m}$ is the bias term. Each attention head is defined as:

$$\mathbf{A}_i = \underbrace{\sigma\,(\frac{\mathbf{Q}_i(\mathbf{K}_i)^{\mathrm{T}}}{\sqrt{d}})}_{\Phi}\,\mathbf{V}_i \tag{1}$$

where

$$\mathbf{Q}_i = \mathbf{X}\mathbf{W}_i^Q + \mathbf{B}_i^Q,$$
$$\mathbf{K}_i = \mathbf{X}\mathbf{W}_i^K + \mathbf{B}_i^K,$$
$$\mathbf{V}_i = \mathbf{X}\mathbf{W}_i^V + \mathbf{B}_i^V,$$

$\mathbf{X} \in \mathbb{R}^{t\times d_m}$ represents input embedding, $\mathbf{W}_i^Q, \mathbf{W}_i^K, \mathbf{W}_i^V \in \mathbb{R}^{d_m\times d}$, $\mathbf{B}_i^Q, \mathbf{B}_i^K, \mathbf{B}_i^V \in \mathbb{R}^{t\times d}$ are bias terms. $d = d_m/h$. σ is the *softmax* function. The input to the *softmax* function can be represented by $\Phi \in \mathbb{R}^{t\times t}$. Because the computational complexity of Φ is $O(t^2)$, which is very expensive, it becomes the main bottleneck of the Transformer model for dealing with long sequences.

Sparse Attention Due to the problem of the original Transformer's attention described above, for long documents, the common practice of previous works (Qiu et al., 2020; Pilault et al., 2020) is to slice the long sequence document into different blocks (which is usually limited to 512 tokens). The downside is that there is no interactive information between the sliced blocks, which causes valuable knowledge loss. Moreover, reducing the input sequence length does not inherently change the algorithm's complexity. In our task, we apply Longformer (Beltagy et al., 2020) to alleviate the computational problem by introducing a sparse attention mechanism consisting of three parts: sliding window attention, dilated sliding window attention, and global sliding window attention.

To be specific, for sliding windows, the $query$ at each location attends only to the $keys$ of the adjacent w locations, which is suitable for capturing the shallow local information. For the dilated sliding window, the $query$ of each position also attends to the $keys$ on w positions, but the position of interest is not adjacent but discontinuous. Dilated sliding attention can attend to non-proximity tokens, which is more suitable for capturing long-distance dependency.

Global attention is identical to the ordinary attention mechanism but only for specific tokens. A token with global attention is associated with every input token. Local tokens attend to the tokens in their own sliding window, and also to all global tokens. The essence of Sparse Attention is to reduce the number of tokens used to compute attention scores, thereby reducing the computational complexity.

2.3 Efficient Fine-Tuning

Most PLMs are highly likely to overfit on the pre-trained data because of the huge amount of parameters. When there is a large domain gap between pre-training and fine-tuning data, the model's parameters are difficult to adjust effectively during fine-tuning (Gao et al., 2021), because: (1) the parameters adjust only slightly during fine-tuning, which is often not sufficient to bridge the domain gap; (2) there is very limited training data for low-resource tasks, making it even harder to adjust many over-fitted parameters.

Parameter Variation To alleviate the first problem, we apply the NoisyTune (Wu et al., 2022)

Size	EFT	R-1	R-2	R-L
original				
2048		30.10	4.50	11.80
full		4.60	1.80	2.70
heuristics				
2048		30.40	4.80	12.10
full		13.60	3.30	6.30
LED				
base		40.80	9.75	16.50
base	BitFit	36.93	8.71	15.42
large		41.51	9.78	16.20
large	BitFit	40.41	10.45	16.37

Table 2: Results of the proposed model on validation set compared to other systems using automatic metrics including ROUGE-1 F1 (R-1), ROUGE-2 F2 (R-2), ROUGE-L F1 (R-L). **EFT** means efficient fine-tuning.

which employs a matrix-level perturbation strategy to increase the variation amplitude of the parameters to adapt the PLMs faster to the target domain on our low-resource data.

Parameter Efficiency Although previous work applied efficient Transformers strategies to reduce the theoretical complexity of the self-attention in long document summarization, how to efficiently utilize PLMs and adapt to new domain data is not explored. Mainly, how to fine-tune large PLMs under exceptionally low-resource settings (1K training samples in our case) using limited hardware resources (Nvidia V100 with 32GB memory) is not well explored. To experiment with parameter efficient fine-tuning method, we also apply BitFit (Ben Zaken et al., 2022), a method that only fine-tunes the bias terms (i.e. $\mathbf{B}^O, \mathbf{B}_i^Q, \mathbf{B}_i^K, \mathbf{B}_i^V$), on a pre-trained LED model checkpoint[2]. By reducing the number of trainable parameters, we aim to increase the fine-tuning speed.

3 Experiments and Analysis

3.1 Experimental Setup

We build our system using HuggingFace transformers (Wolf et al., 2019) and train LED on the training split of the Scriptbase dataset. We choose the checkpoint before over-fitting for evaluation. We limit the output length between 512 and 1024 tokens. For the rest, we follow the configuration from Longformer (Beltagy et al., 2020).

All experiments is optimized using AdamW (Loshchilov and Hutter, 2017) (where β_1 was 0.9, β_2 was 0.99, ϵ was 1e-8) and the initial learning rate is set to 5e-5 with weight decay of 0.01. The number of warm-up steps is 512. We enable mixed precision during training and evaluation to save memory for larger batch size. We use ROUGE in evaluation on validation split. All ROUGE scores are multiplied by 100.

3.2 Hidden Test Submission

For the test submission, we train our models on the training and validation splits of the Scriptbase dataset following the organizers' instructions. We train all the models either in pure fine-tuning or coupling with *NoisyTune* or *BitFit* method. Hence, we obtain 3 systems: `UdS`, `UdS NoisyTune` and `UdS BitFit` respectively.

For the sake of fairness, the results on the unseen test set are released by the organizing committee as shown in Table 1. Compared with the official baseline models, all candidate models have improved in various metrics. Particularly, `UdS NoisyTune` that introduces noise during fine-tuning performs the best overall. Among them, 6 of the 9 evaluation metrics achieved the best performance. The competitor's model (MovING) outperforms ours only on the SummaCZS metric (Laban et al., 2022), which is an evaluation metric that focuses on inconsistency in summaries. Furthermore, `UdS BitFit` that applies the BitFit algorithm to fine-tune only 0.09% of the parameters is very close to the `UdS` performance, but its more significant advantages lie in fewer computational parameters and shorter training time.

3.3 Baseline Comparison

Unfortunately, no previous work reports standard summarization metrics (like ROUGE) on the Scriptbase dataset (Gorinski and Lapata, 2015; Papalampidi et al., 2019, 2021; Lee et al., 2021). We therefore create a *naive* baseline by copying first M tokens from source sequence. We apply this baseline to both the original movie scripts (*original*) and the extracted texts using our heuristics (*heuristics*). As we increase M from 128 by a factor of 2 up until the length of the source text, we observe that the recall of ROUGE-1/2/L increase and the precision decrease as expected. We thus report the *naive* baseline with the highest F1 (2048) and with input full length in Table 2. Results show that the *naive* baseline using our heuristics outperforms the

[2]https://huggingface.co/allenai/led-base-16384

Input	Avg. Len.	Input Len.	%	R-2-P	R-2-R	R-2-F1
all	24106	8192	100%	10.46	11.34	10.26
all	24106	16384	100%	11.26	12.05	11.02
dialogue	15818	8192	66%	10.67	11.71	10.52
dialogue	15818	16384	66%	10.39	12.78	10.90
ours	8288	8192	34%	10.47	11.91	10.52

Table 3: Results of the model trained on data created with our heuristics extraction method compared to other extraction methods.

Models	Output
Gold	MI6 sends James Bond, agent 007, into the field to spy on a terrorist arms bazaar on the Russian border. Via television, MI6 and the Royal Navy identify several wanted men, including American "techno-terrorist" Henry Gupta, who is buying a GPS encoder made by the U.S. military...
BART	The film is being shot by the British pilot, as he attempts to escape, but is shot by a group of a helicopter. He is killed by a helicopter pilot, the helicopter. The pilot from the pilot who has a helicopter which the helicopter pilot who is killed...
T5	James Bond is a former MI6 operative, now working for MI-6. He was assigned to spy on Russian President Vladimir Vladimirovich Kirillov's election campaign. Bond is assigned to investigate the uranium scandal in Vladivostok....
Our	James Bond is a British Secret Service agent, nicknamed "Bond", who works for MI6. He is recruited by M, the head of the agency's counter-espionage unit, to investigate the disappearance of highly enriched uranium from a UK nuclear reactor...

Table 4: Case study of model-generated output. More examples can be found in our GitHub repo.

baseline using original text under the optimal setting (2048) and under the full length setting (full)[3].

3.4 Model Selection

Prior state-of-the-art Transformer models either fail to handle such long-range movie scripts or perform slowly during training time. For example, the maximum input length of BART (Lewis et al., 2020), PEGASUS (Zhang et al., 2020), T5 (Raffel et al., 2020) and BigBird (Zaheer et al., 2020) are all less than 4096. Among BART, T5 and LED, our benchmark comparison shows that LED achieves strong performance compared to BART by 2.4 points and is 8× times faster than T5 at the training stage. We thus develop our system based on LED. The detailed comparison is in Appendix A. We extend the original LED with two recent fine-tuning methods, BitFit and NoisyTune. Both model variations with these techniques achieve strong results on R-2 F1 scores. In addition, we set the encoding length as 8192 and the decoding length 1024 with beam size 4 (BS) for all our experiments. Figure 5 shows that UdS BitFit stops the performance improvement when $BS > 4$, but with a huge time complexity. Hence, we choose $BS = 4$.

[3]Figure 5 in Appendix B further shows that our submitted system outperforms all *naive* baselines by a large margin.

3.5 Case Study

Table 4 shows the first two sentences of the movie summary of "Tomorrow Never Dies" in the dataset. Where Gold is the human answer, we compared the output of our model with the current SOAT model BART and T5. We find that our model can effectively capture proper nouns in movies, such as characters, organizations, locations, etc., and the generated sentences are more in line with a reasonable story logic. However, the BART model seems to only be able to focus on a certain part of the plot in the movie and cannot summarize the movie well. T5 model often generates sentences that contradict the truth and has difficulty handling transitions between sentences.

3.6 Ablation Study

Input Data To further show the effectiveness of our heuristics extraction method, we conduct an ablation study where we train our best summarization model with three different inputs: the full movie scripts (all), the actions and dialogues that are selected by our heuristics (ours), and the dialogues that are omitted by our heuristics (dialogue). We also experiment with two input lengths (8192 and 16384). Results in Table 3 demonstrate that our heuristics extraction method reduces the input length significantly down to 33% of the original length with only 4.5% performance loss compared to the model using full scripts (all).

Performance and Decoding Time Trade-off To understand the dependency between model performance and runtime, we conduct the ablation study of testing the evaluation runtime when varying the beam size (BS). Figure 2 illustrates that UdS BitFit stops showing significant improvement in performance after $BS = 4$ but takes more decoding time than the total training time (red dotted line). Using large BS from 5 to 8 requires additional 1 to 6 hours yet only obtains 0 to 2% performance gain. This indicates the decoding with large BS

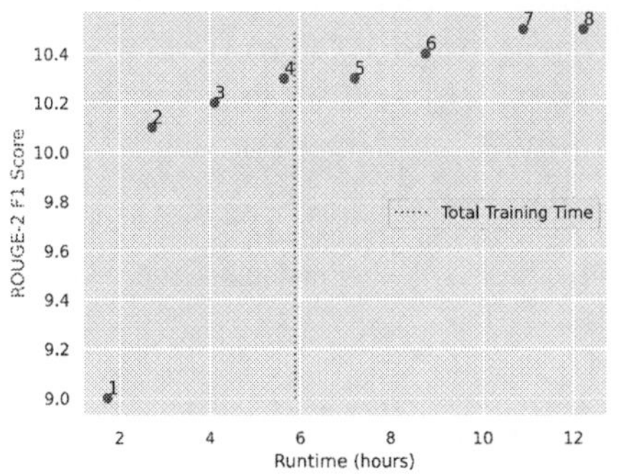

Figure 2: Performance (blue points) and evaluation runtime (hours) of UdS BitFit when varying in beam sizes (BS) from 1 to 8. The points are labeled with their BS. The total training time is marked by red dotted line. All UdS BitFit models are evaluated on the validation set.

is extremely expensive but unnecessary. We also provide further analysis to understand the impact of encoding and decoding lengths on performance and runtime in Appendix B.

4 Related Work

4.1 Efficient Transformers

Transformer-based models (Vaswani et al., 2017) are widely applied for text generation problems, but the $O(n^2)$ complexity of the attention calculation makes long document text generation computationally expensive and prohibitive. Various strategies have been proposed to ameliorate this issue (Correia et al., 2019; Child et al., 2019; Beltagy et al., 2020; Guo et al., 2022; Tay et al., 2020; Ainslie et al., 2020; Zaheer et al., 2020; Wang et al., 2020; Peng et al., 2020b; Dai et al., 2019). Most of these proposals demonstrate efficiency of their model on Long Range Arena (LRA), a benchmark of six simple tasks to evaluate the efficiency of different Transformers (Tay et al., 2021). However, only one of these tasks (Path-X) has an input length of 16K which is much longer than the input lengths of the other five tasks (mostly below 10K), and most of these methods failed on Path-X. Thus it is unclear whether the good performance on LRA can be transferred to more realistic downstream tasks like long-document summarization.

4.2 Long Document Summarization

Long document summarization is a trending natural language generation task. Existing solutions are principally divided into two directions: The first is a multi-stage strategy that reduces long input sequences while minimizing the loss of important details (Moro and Ragazzi, 2022; Zhang et al., 2022). The second improves the internal representation of the summarization model to process longer inputs efficiently (Zhang et al., 2020; Xiao et al., 2022; Mao et al., 2022; Cao and Wang, 2022). However, the above strategies are either domain-specific or pre-training corrections. Few people have explored effective fine-tuning strategies for long sequence large models in text summarization tasks, and the main content of our work is to fill this gap.

5 Conclusion

In this paper, we present the details of our system, which ranks 1st in the Scriptbase track on various metrics, including ROUGE, BERTScore, and N-gram diversities. We show that the proposed approach involving a two-stage solution results in competitive and efficient performance for long-form text encoding and generation. In addition, we deliver analysis and ablation studies for the components within our proposed techniques, which allows us to draw further conclusions about decoding configurations and vocabulary sampling. Lastly, we argue that more work can be done to speed up the model selection process, which impacts the model performance and model training and evaluation.

Acknowledgements

This project has received funding from the European Research Council (ERC) under the European Union's Horizon 2020 research and innovation programme (grant agreement No 948878). Xudong Hong is supported by the International Max Planck Research School for Computer Science (IMPRS-CS) of Max-Planck Institute for Informatics (MPI-INF).

erc
European Research Council
Established by the European Commission

References

Joshua Ainslie, Santiago Ontanon, Chris Alberti, Vaclav Cvicek, Zachary Fisher, Philip Pham, Anirudh Ravula, Sumit Sanghai, Qifan Wang, and Li Yang. 2020. ETC: Encoding long and structured inputs in transformers. In *Proceedings of the 2020 Conference on Empirical Methods in Natural Language Processing (EMNLP)*, pages 268–284, Online. Association for Computational Linguistics.

Imen Akermi, Johannes Heinecke, and Frédéric Herledan. 2020. Transformer based natural language generation for question-answering. In *Proceedings of the 13th International Conference on Natural Language Generation*, pages 349–359, Dublin, Ireland. Association for Computational Linguistics.

Iz Beltagy, Matthew E Peters, and Arman Cohan. 2020. Longformer: The long-document transformer. *arXiv preprint arXiv:2004.05150*.

Elad Ben Zaken, Yoav Goldberg, and Shauli Ravfogel. 2022. BitFit: Simple parameter-efficient fine-tuning for transformer-based masked language-models. In *Proceedings of the 60th Annual Meeting of the Association for Computational Linguistics (Volume 2: Short Papers)*, pages 1–9, Dublin, Ireland. Association for Computational Linguistics.

Shuyang Cao and Lu Wang. 2022. HIBRIDS: Attention with hierarchical biases for structure-aware long document summarization. In *Proceedings of the 60th Annual Meeting of the Association for Computational Linguistics (Volume 1: Long Papers)*, pages 786–807, Dublin, Ireland. Association for Computational Linguistics.

Rewon Child, Scott Gray, Alec Radford, and Ilya Sutskever. 2019. Generating long sequences with sparse transformers. *arXiv preprint arXiv:1904.10509*.

Gonçalo M. Correia, Vlad Niculae, and André F. T. Martins. 2019. Adaptively sparse transformers. In *Proceedings of the 2019 Conference on Empirical Methods in Natural Language Processing and the 9th International Joint Conference on Natural Language Processing (EMNLP-IJCNLP)*, pages 2174–2184, Hong Kong, China. Association for Computational Linguistics.

Zihang Dai, Zhilin Yang, Yiming Yang, Jaime Carbonell, Quoc Le, and Ruslan Salakhutdinov. 2019. Transformer-XL: Attentive language models beyond a fixed-length context. In *Proceedings of the 57th Annual Meeting of the Association for Computational Linguistics*, pages 2978–2988, Florence, Italy. Association for Computational Linguistics.

Erkut Erdem, Menekse Kuyu, Semih Yagcioglu, Anette Frank, Letitia Parcalabescu, Barbara Plank, Andrii Babii, Oleksii Turuta, Aykut Erdem, Iacer Calixto, et al. 2022. Neural natural language generation: A survey on multilinguality, multimodality, controllability and learning. *Journal of Artificial Intelligence Research*, 73:1131–1207.

Tianyu Gao, Adam Fisch, and Danqi Chen. 2021. Making pre-trained language models better few-shot learners. In *Proceedings of the 59th Annual Meeting of the Association for Computational Linguistics and the 11th International Joint Conference on Natural Language Processing (Volume 1: Long Papers)*, pages 3816–3830, Online. Association for Computational Linguistics.

Philip John Gorinski and Mirella Lapata. 2015. Movie script summarization as graph-based scene extraction. In *Proceedings of the 2015 Conference of the North American Chapter of the Association for Computational Linguistics: Human Language Technologies*, pages 1066–1076, Denver, Colorado. Association for Computational Linguistics.

Mandy Guo, Joshua Ainslie, David Uthus, Santiago Ontanon, Jianmo Ni, Yun-Hsuan Sung, and Yinfei Yang. 2022. LongT5: Efficient text-to-text transformer for long sequences. In *Findings of the Association for Computational Linguistics: NAACL 2022*, pages 724–736, Seattle, United States. Association for Computational Linguistics.

Philippe Laban, Tobias Schnabel, Paul N. Bennett, and Marti A. Hearst. 2022. SummaC: Re-visiting NLI-based models for inconsistency detection in summarization. *Transactions of the Association for Computational Linguistics*, 10:163–177.

Myungji Lee, Hongseok Kwon, Jaehun Shin, Won-Kee Lee, Baikjin Jung, and Jong-Hyeok Lee. 2021. Transformer-based screenplay summarization using augmented learning representation with dialogue information. In *Proceedings of the Third Workshop on Narrative Understanding*, pages 56–61, Virtual. Association for Computational Linguistics.

Mike Lewis, Yinhan Liu, Naman Goyal, Marjan Ghazvininejad, Abdelrahman Mohamed, Omer Levy, Veselin Stoyanov, and Luke Zettlemoyer. 2020. BART: Denoising sequence-to-sequence pre-training for natural language generation, translation, and comprehension. In *Proceedings of the 58th Annual Meeting of the Association for Computational Linguistics*, pages 7871–7880, Online. Association for Computational Linguistics.

Ilya Loshchilov and Frank Hutter. 2017. Decoupled weight decay regularization. *arXiv preprint arXiv:1711.05101*.

Ziming Mao, Chen Henry Wu, Ansong Ni, Yusen Zhang, Rui Zhang, Tao Yu, Budhaditya Deb, Chenguang Zhu, Ahmed Awadallah, and Dragomir Radev. 2022. DYLE: Dynamic latent extraction for abstractive long-input summarization. In *Proceedings of the 60th Annual Meeting of the Association for Computational Linguistics (Volume 1: Long Papers)*, pages 1687–1698, Dublin, Ireland. Association for Computational Linguistics.

Gianluca Moro and Luca Ragazzi. 2022. Semantic self-segmentation for abstractive summarization of long legal documents in low-resource regimes. In *Proceedings of the Thirty-Six AAAI Conference on Artificial Intelligence, Virtual*, volume 22.

Pinelopi Papalampidi, Frank Keller, and Mirella Lapata. 2019. Movie plot analysis via turning point identification. In *Proceedings of the 2019 Conference on Empirical Methods in Natural Language Processing and the 9th International Joint Conference on Natural Language Processing (EMNLP-IJCNLP)*, pages 1707–1717, Hong Kong, China. Association for Computational Linguistics.

Pinelopi Papalampidi, Frank Keller, and Mirella Lapata. 2021. Movie summarization via sparse graph construction. In *AAAI*.

Baolin Peng, Chenguang Zhu, Chunyuan Li, Xiujun Li, Jinchao Li, Michael Zeng, and Jianfeng Gao. 2020a. Few-shot natural language generation for task-oriented dialog. In *Findings of the Association for Computational Linguistics: EMNLP 2020*, pages 172–182, Online. Association for Computational Linguistics.

Hao Peng, Nikolaos Pappas, Dani Yogatama, Roy Schwartz, Noah Smith, and Lingpeng Kong. 2020b. Random feature attention. In *International Conference on Learning Representations*.

Jonathan Pilault, Raymond Li, Sandeep Subramanian, and Chris Pal. 2020. On extractive and abstractive neural document summarization with transformer language models. In *Proceedings of the 2020 Conference on Empirical Methods in Natural Language Processing (EMNLP)*, pages 9308–9319, Online. Association for Computational Linguistics.

Jing Qian, Li Dong, Yelong Shen, Furu Wei, and Weizhu Chen. 2022. Controllable natural language generation with contrastive prefixes. In *Findings of the Association for Computational Linguistics: ACL 2022*, pages 2912–2924, Dublin, Ireland. Association for Computational Linguistics.

Jiezhong Qiu, Hao Ma, Omer Levy, Wen-tau Yih, Sinong Wang, and Jie Tang. 2020. Blockwise self-attention for long document understanding. In *Findings of the Association for Computational Linguistics: EMNLP 2020*, pages 2555–2565, Online. Association for Computational Linguistics.

Colin Raffel, Noam Shazeer, Adam Roberts, Katherine Lee, Sharan Narang, Michael Matena, Yanqi Zhou, Wei Li, Peter J Liu, et al. 2020. Exploring the limits of transfer learning with a unified text-to-text transformer. *J. Mach. Learn. Res.*, 21(140):1–67.

Yi Tay, Dara Bahri, Liu Yang, Donald Metzler, and Da-Cheng Juan. 2020. Sparse sinkhorn attention. In *International Conference on Machine Learning*, pages 9438–9447. PMLR.

Yi Tay, Mostafa Dehghani, Samira Abnar, Yikang Shen, Dara Bahri, Philip Pham, Jinfeng Rao, Liu Yang, Sebastian Ruder, and Donald Metzler. 2021. Long range arena: A benchmark for efficient transformers. In *International Conference on Learning Representations*.

Ashish Vaswani, Noam Shazeer, Niki Parmar, Jakob Uszkoreit, Llion Jones, Aidan N Gomez, Łukasz Kaiser, and Illia Polosukhin. 2017. Attention is all you need. *Advances in neural information processing systems*, 30.

Sinong Wang, Belinda Z Li, Madian Khabsa, Han Fang, and Hao Ma. 2020. Linformer: Self-attention with linear complexity. *arXiv preprint arXiv:2006.04768*.

Thomas Wolf, Lysandre Debut, Victor Sanh, Julien Chaumond, Clement Delangue, Anthony Moi, Pierric Cistac, Tim Rault, Rémi Louf, Morgan Funtowicz, et al. 2019. Huggingface's transformers: State-of-the-art natural language processing. *arXiv preprint arXiv:1910.03771*.

Chuhan Wu, Fangzhao Wu, Tao Qi, and Yongfeng Huang. 2022. NoisyTune: A little noise can help you finetune pretrained language models better. In *Proceedings of the 60th Annual Meeting of the Association for Computational Linguistics (Volume 2: Short Papers)*, pages 680–685, Dublin, Ireland. Association for Computational Linguistics.

Wen Xiao, Iz Beltagy, Giuseppe Carenini, and Arman Cohan. 2022. PRIMERA: Pyramid-based masked sentence pre-training for multi-document summarization. In *Proceedings of the 60th Annual Meeting of the Association for Computational Linguistics (Volume 1: Long Papers)*, pages 5245–5263, Dublin, Ireland. Association for Computational Linguistics.

Manzil Zaheer, Guru Guruganesh, Kumar Avinava Dubey, Joshua Ainslie, Chris Alberti, Santiago Ontanon, Philip Pham, Anirudh Ravula, Qifan Wang, Li Yang, et al. 2020. Big bird: Transformers for longer sequences. *Advances in Neural Information Processing Systems*, 33:17283–17297.

Jingqing Zhang, Yao Zhao, Mohammad Saleh, and Peter Liu. 2020. Pegasus: Pre-training with extracted gap-sentences for abstractive summarization. In *International Conference on Machine Learning*, pages 11328–11339. PMLR.

Yusen Zhang, Ansong Ni, Ziming Mao, Chen Henry Wu, Chenguang Zhu, Budhaditya Deb, Ahmed Awadallah, Dragomir Radev, and Rui Zhang. 2022. Summ^n: A multi-stage summarization framework for long input dialogues and documents. In *Proceedings of the 60th Annual Meeting of the Association for Computational Linguistics (Volume 1: Long Papers)*, pages 1592–1604, Dublin, Ireland. Association for Computational Linguistics.

A Appendix: Benchmark Comparison

Table 5 compares current state-of-the-art Transformer-based models to find the optimal model architecture. For BART, we extend input length up to 5120 until total memory footprints can be loaded into one Nvidia Tesla V100 with

Architecure	# Tok.	T	R-2-F1
BART	5K	1	6.30
T5	8K	16	8.60
LED	8K	2	**8.70**

Table 5: Comparison of model architectures. BART, T5 and LED are trained for 10 epochs. $\#Tok.$: the number of tokens as the maximum input length to the encoder. T: the training time in hours. All models are in base size and evaluated on validation set and use decoding length 1024.

32 GB. Because BART is not designed to handle such long-form sequences, we extend the size of position embeddings by initializing from the pre-trained position embeddings in BART. For T5 and LED, we use the input length ($\#Tok.$) 8192 to encode whole movie scripts. Lastly, we fine-tune all models for 10 epochs and report the ROUGE-2 F1 score (R-2-F1) on the validation set. Based on the finding of the ablation study on beam size (Sec. 3.6), all experiments use $BS = 4$.

Among the current SOTA models: BART, T5 and LED, we obtain 6.3 and 8.6 and 8.7 on R-2 F1 scores respectively. For the performance, LED outperforms BART and T5 by 2.4 and 0.1 points. The demand of high complexity attention computation in BART limits the maximum input length and thus fails to generalise well on the long-form movie summarization. On the other hand, employing to global sliding window attention, LED does not need to shrink its input context length and greatly benefits from 16-bit mixed precision training by which take only 2 hours. In contrast, fine-tuning T5 requires 32-bit training which results in 8× slower than LED at training phase. Based on the performance and training efficiency advantages, we leverage LED for the development of our long-form summarization system on CreativeSumm'22.

B Appendix: Runtime Performance

To further understand the effects of different encoding and decoding lengths on model performance to select models and its inference efficiency, we design the controlled trails to test the impact of encoding and decoding lengths. We use our performant UdS NoisyTune and evaluate model on validation set using $BS = 4$.

Impact of Encoding Lengths Figure 3 shows the dependency between performance (blue) and runtime (red) on various encoding length. It is

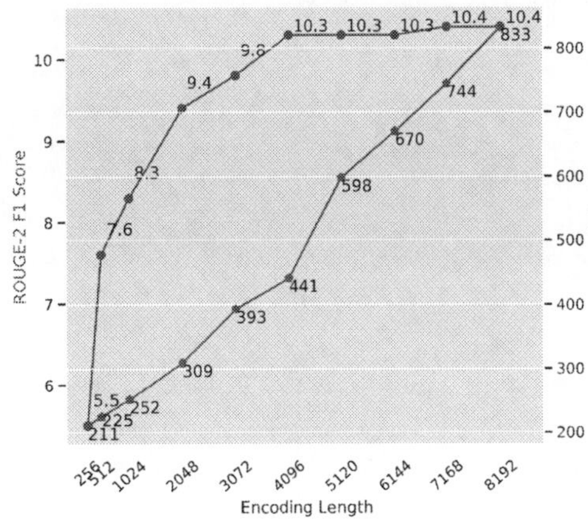

Figure 3: Performance (blue) and decoding runtime (red) when varying in encoding lengths. We report the ROUGE-2 F1 score and inference time on various input lengths from 256 up to 8192.

worth noting that the model is to be performant only when it encodes a long enough movie script, such as $8K$. More importantly, we reduced input length to 4094 with only 0.1 performance drops.

However, the runtime varying in different encoding lengths and scales linearly as encoding length increases. These results suggest that the current Transformer-based encoder-decoder model with quadratic-form attention would be even worse at inference.

Impact of Decoding Lengths Unlike the encoding length, the decoding length plays a more critical role in the inference time. The performance gradually drops caused by shorter decoding length which is making sense as the length of gold summary is around $1K$.

Notably, runtime varying in decoding length follows a quadratic trend. By shrinking decoding length to 768, we find that the summarizer obtains 1.6× speedups at inference time while keeping 96% performance. In addition, by reducing decoding length to 512, our model achieves 3.3× speedups and keeps 89% performance on the R-2 F1 score. Our result indicates that reducing decoding length to 75% or 50% of the original decoding length significantly improves its inference efficiency without much performance drops.

Impact of Beam Size To understand the dependency between model performance and runtime when varying beam sizes (BS), Figure 5 illustrates

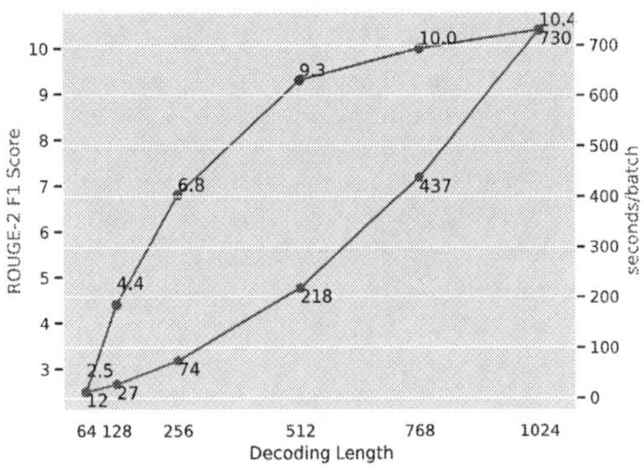

Figure 4: Performance (blue) and decoding runtime (red) when varying in decoding lengths. We report the ROUGE-2 F1 score and inference time on various output lengths from 64 up to 1024.

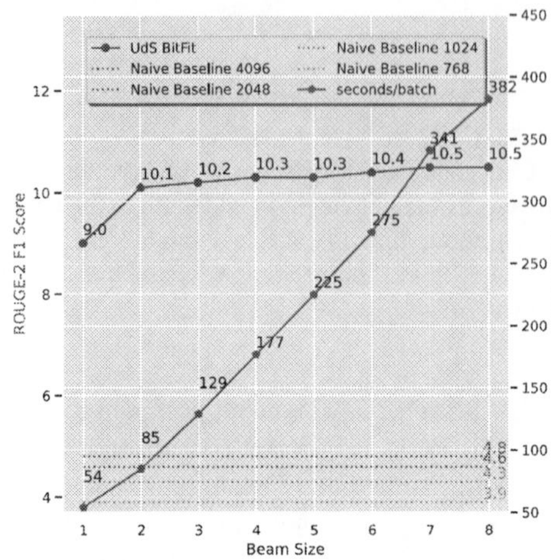

Figure 5: Performance (blue) and runtime (red) of UdS BitFit when varying in beam sizes. We evaluate UdS BitFit on various beam size (BS) from 1 to 8. All models are evaluated on validation set.

the performance between our system (blue) , *naive* baselines (dotted lines) and inference speed (red). As choosing $BS = 2$, UdS BitFit gains 3.4 points improvement compared to the model using greedy search ($BS = 1$) on ROUGE-2 F1 score. In addition, our UdS BitFit using large BS from 4 to 8 achieve the best performance 14.9 and significantly outperforms the *naive* baseline 2048 by 10.1 points on the ROUGE-2 F1 score. The result suggests $BS = 4$ is sufficient to obtain the most performant result.

However, the runtime scales linearly with the BS increasing. For instance, UdS BitFit stops showing the improvement in performance after $BS = 4$ but takes more computational cost. Using large BS from 5 to 8 requires around 5 to 8 minutes for merely one mini-batch (size=1), which shows the decoding with large BS is extremely expensive.

C Appendix: Background

C.1 Efficient Transformers

Transformer-based models (Vaswani et al., 2017) are widely applied for text generation problems but the $O(n^2)$ complexity of the self-attention makes long document text generation computationally expensive and prohibitive. Various strategies have been proposed to address this issue: **1.** Complexity can be reduced by restricting the global attention to local patterns. (Correia et al., 2019) learn shorter attention patterns for different heads and different layers, (Child et al., 2019; Beltagy et al., 2020; Guo et al., 2022) use random, stride or fixed local attention patterns, (Tay et al., 2020) use learnable attention patterns improve the memory efficiency of the attention module. **2.** (Ainslie et al., 2020; Zaheer et al., 2020) use memory/downsampling methods. **3.** Complexity can also be reduced by approximating self-attention using low-rank decomposition (Wang et al., 2020) or kernels (Peng et al., 2020b). **4.** The context of transformers can also be encoded into a fixed sized hidden state (Dai et al., 2019).

CREATIVESUMM: Shared Task on Automatic Summarization for Creative Writing

Divyansh Agarwal[1] **Alexander R. Fabbri**[1] **Simeng Han**[3] **Wojciech Kryściński**[1]
Faisal Ladhak[2] **Bryan Li**[5] **Kathleen McKeown**[2]
Dragomir Radev[3] **Tianyi Zhang**[4] **Sam Wiseman**[6]
[1]Salesforce Research [2]Columbia University [3]Yale University
[4]Stanford University [5]University of Pennsylvania [6]Duke University

Abstract

This paper introduces the shared task of summarizing documents in several creative domains, namely literary texts, movie scripts, and television scripts. Summarizing these creative documents requires making complex literary interpretations, as well as understanding non-trivial temporal dependencies in texts containing varied styles of plot development and narrative structure. This poses unique challenges and is yet underexplored for text summarization systems. In this shared task, we introduce four sub-tasks and their corresponding datasets, focusing on summarizing books, movie scripts, primetime television scripts, and daytime soap opera scripts. We detail the process of curating these datasets for the task, as well as the metrics used for the evaluation of the submissions. As part of the CREATIVESUMM workshop at COLING 2022, the shared task attracted 18 submissions in total. We discuss the submissions and the baselines for each sub-task in this paper, along with directions for facilitating future work.

1 Introduction

Contemporary research in text summarization systems has focused mainly on a select few domains such as news, scientific and legal articles. While summarizing these domains is important, the corresponding documents are limited in length and the diversity of the discourse structure.

There is a large body of creative texts available on the web that pose greater challenges for text summarization in NLP. These creative documents like books, movie scripts, and television scripts are usually written by 'subject matter experts', are substantial in length and contain complex inter-dependencies between characters in the plotline (Kryscinski et al., 2021; Ladhak et al., 2020; Mihalcea and Ceylan, 2007). Summarization of such text requires understanding many different genres, and offers the possibility of improving creating writing platforms (Aparício et al., 2016; Toubia, 2021; Gorinski and Lapata, 2015).

Such creative documents are often accompanied by a synopses, short-description or a summary, which allows readers to gauge their interest in the corresponding artifact. Summaries of creative texts are widely used by students as study guides, and could be useful to experts that need to grade the quality of these documents for a particular audience. Furthermore, researchers may be interested in using the challenges posed by these creative texts, to identify the limitations of large language models at understanding complex discourse structure.

To further summarization research of creative writing, we identified four particular domains, each with their own set of challenges. Building off of datasets recently released in the community, we develop a shared task, composed of four sub-tasks, and encouraged participants to further research in this direction.

For sub-task 1, we focus on summarization of chapters from literary texts like books, novels and stories. We curate a combined version of Booksum (Kryscinski et al., 2021) and NovelChapters (Ladhak et al., 2020) for this purpose.

For sub-task 2, we use the Scriptbase dataset (Gorinski and Lapata, 2015), which pairs movie transcripts with their corresponding Wikipedia summaries.

Sub-tasks 3 and 4 both relate to summarization of transcripts for TV shows, both derived from SummScreen (Chen et al., 2021), which contains two non-overlapping set of TV shows, from different sources. The two sources provide transcripts for two different domains - prime time TV shows and daytime 'soap operas', respectively forming the sub-task 3 and 4.

We share the instructions to access the data for each of the four sub-tasks and associated scripts on

Proceedings of the 58th Annual Meeting of the Association for Computational Linguistics, pages 67–73
July 5–10, 2020. ©2020 Association for Computational Linguistics
https://doi.org/10.26615/978-954-452-056-4_010

our github repo [1].

We detail the process of evaluation of these sub-tasks, presenting the metrics as well as the results from the submissions by the shared-task participants alongside several baseline, long-document summarization models. We discuss ways to expand the sub-tasks to include more genres of creative writing for automatic summarization systems in the future.

2 Datasets

In this section we describe the sources and pre-processing steps taken to curate the data from each sub-task of CREATIVESUMM. The data samples for each of the sub-tasks are available on the shared task github repo.

2.1 Sub-Task 1: Summarizing book chapters

The dataset for sub-task 1 (*BookSumm-chapters*) pairs chapters of novels released as part of Project Gutenberg with corresponding summaries from different online study guides. Source texts for these chapters have been made available in accordance with Project Gutenberg's guidelines. [2] For each book-chapter, we provide a link to the online study guide on Web Archive[3] where the corresponding ground truth summary can be found, for training and validation.

We combine the book titles and the study guide sources used by Kryscinski et al. (2021) and Ladhak et al. (2020), and ensure that we remove redundant titles and filter out unreliable study guides. We also filter out book-chapters that were identified as plays (such as those by Shakespeare), as they differ significantly from the other literary genres in the dataset. The book titles in each of our resulting data splits are non-overlapping.

2.2 Sub-Task 2: Summarizing movie transcripts

Scriptbase (Gorinski and Lapata, 2015) compiles a corpus of 1276 movie scripts/screenplays spanning 1909–2013, by crawling relevant web-sites. They pair the scripts with corresponding user-written summaries for the task of summarizing movie transcripts. The movie scripts comprise 23 different genres, and also include rich information about the multimodal aspects of the various scenes. The authors introduce the task of summarizing movie transcripts, as selecting a chain of scenes that accurately represents a film's story. In addition to the original Scriptbase data, we provide a *new* test set containing transcripts and summaries that did not appear in the original Scriptbase release.

2.3 Sub-Task 3: Summarizing transcripts from primetime tv-shows

We utilize the SummScreen dataset (Chen et al., 2021) for the task of summarizing transcripts of episodes from primetime tv-shows. The dataset (*SummScreenFD*) contains community-contributed transcripts for 4348 episodes from 88 shows, gathered from ForeverDreaming (FD).[4] The transcripts are paired with human-written summaries. These transcripts are characterized by long storylines, often involving parallel sub-plots and with great emphasis on character development. For this subtask, we use the data and pre-processing associated with the SCROLLS benchmark (Shaham et al., 2022), but we provide a *new* test set containing transcripts and summaries not released in either the original SummScreen or SCROLLS datasets.

2.4 Sub-Task 4: Summarizing transcripts from daytime 'soap-operas'

The dataset for sub-task 4 is made available in the exact same format as 2.3, except the transcripts are specific to daytime 'soap opera' type shows. Introduced by Chen et al. (2021), *SummScreenTMS* contains transcripts from 22.5k episodes, from TV MegaSite, Inc. (TMS).[5] Here again we provide a *new* test set containing transcripts and summaries not released in the original SummScreen dataset.

2.5 Data Splits

As noted above, while we used the original data splits for Sub-Task 1, we provided new unseen test inputs for Sub-Tasks 2, 3 & 4. For *SummScreenFD* & *SummScreenTMS* we suggested participants use the original test set for validation, and train on the combination of the original train and validation sets. We provide the data splits and some statistics for each sub-task in Table 1.

3 Evaluation

We received 18 submissions in total for our shared task, with two, eleven, three and two submissions

[1] github.com/fladhak/creative-summ-data

[2] https://www.gutenberg.org/policy/robot_access.html

[3] https://web.archive.org/

[4] transcripts.foreverdreaming.org

[5] http://tvmegasite.net/

Dataset	Train	Val	Test	Coverage	Density	Comp. Ratio	1-grams	2-grams
BookSumm-chapters	6754	983	851	0.7062	1.4078	16.4287	0.4456	0.8163
Scriptbase	1149	127	216	0.7637	1.2624	63.2474	0.3123	0.667
SummScreenFD	4011	337	459	0.7203	1.1138	87.5306	0.2640	0.7066
SummScreenTMS	20710	1793	679	0.7665	1.1954	21.0675	0.2499	0.6969

Table 1: Statistics of the documents in the dataset curated for each sub-task. We report the number of documents in each split, along with the coverage, density and compression ratio b/w the documents and the summaries in the full dataset. We also present the percentage of novel uni and bi-grams present in the reference summaries for documents in each sub-task.

for shared tasks 1, 2, 3 and 4 respectively. We describe the metrics used for evaluating the submitted outputs. Participants had 12 weeks to sign up for the shared task and train their models, before we released the test set(s) for the different sub-tasks. We allowed another week after releasing the test set for the submission of system outputs. We encouraged multiple submissions for each sub-task as long as they reflected different models or approaches.

3.1 Metrics

We used the same metrics for the evaluation of the four sub-tasks for easier comparison:

ROUGE (Lin, 2004): We apply the standard F1 variations of ROUGE-1, ROUGE-2, and ROUGE-L using the original PERL-based implementation.

BERTScore (Zhang et al., 2020): We compute the precision, recall, and F1 variations of reference-based BERTScore metric. We provide the hash of our BERTScore runs. [6]

LitePyramid (LP) (Zhang and Bansal, 2021): This metric has reported state-of-the-art correlations for relevance estimation on news summarization. This metric is fully automatic and first extracts semantic textual units from the reference summaries and then calculates the entailment score between the model summary and these units. We report the three-class entailment probability using an entailment model fine-tuned on TAC 2008 (TAC).

SummaC (Laban et al., 2022): We chose this metric as it relies on aggregating sentence-level computations, allowing us to score long input texts. We use zero-shot variation of the model, whose NLI component is trained on the VitaminC dataset (Schuster et al., 2021).

Summary Statistics: We report the average length and percentage of novel uni and bi-grams present in the model summaries. We also calculate the extractive coverage and density from Grusky et al. (2018), which measure the extent of the overlap between the summary and input texts.

3.2 Baselines

For each sub-task, we train three Longformer Encoder-Decoder (LED) (Beltagy et al., 2020) models that have a maximum input size of 1024, 4096, and 16384, respectively.

3.3 Results

The results for each of the sub-tasks are presented in Appendix A.

The submissions on all tasks surpass the performance of the baseline LED models by a large margin in terms of ROUGE and BERTScore. However, baselines and submissions score poorly in LP and SummaC, with several system scores near zero. These two metrics have been primarily studied within the news domain and with relatively short input, and additional analysis is required to validate these metrics within creative writing and longer input/output summarization.

Within the *BookSum-chapters* dataset, we find a sizable variation in the length and level of abstraction among systems. We also note that among the tasks, LP and SummaC give the highest scores to the systems here. Notably, we do not see a clear correspondence between the level of abstraction and the SummaC factual consistency score, which has often been observed in the news domain (Ladhak et al., 2022).

For the *Scriptbase* task, we received many variations of a base model from one team with different performance, although the gap between system statistics is not very large. The ROUGE performance on this dataset is highest among all tasks, although we again note the low performance of all systems according to LP and SummaC.

For the *SummScreenFD* task, the system that performed best consisted of much shorter, fairly abstractive summaries. For the *SummScreenTMS*

[6] microsoft/deberta-xlarge-mnli_L40_no-idf_version=0.3.9(hug_trans=4.20.1)

task, the LED baselines perform very poorly, and we found the output to be largely repetitive, likely due to optimization problems during training. The resulting baselines were much longer and more extractive than the submitted systems. The difference in system performance on the two SummScreen tasks (0.29 vs. 0.39 ROUGE-1 on SummScreen FD and TMS, respectively) demonstrates important data differences even within the same domain.

4 Related Work

Although summarization of newswire text has dominated research for over a decade, there have been key efforts at encouraging summarizing research in other domains. Nenkova et al. (2011) introduced a workshop on summarizing different genres, media and languages, with the aim of defining new tasks and corporas in these domains.

Toubia (2017) and Toubia (2021) highlight the need for summarization of creative documents, by arguing that summaries may serve as a "lubricant" in the market for creative content, making it easier for consumers to decide which information to consume.

TVRecap (Chen and Gimpel, 2021) introduced a story generation task that requires generating detailed recaps from a brief summary and a set of documents describing the characters involved in the episode. The dataset contains 26k episode recaps of TV shows gathered from fan-contributed websites.

Past work has demonstrated the importance of character analysis for understanding and summarizing the content of movie scripts (Sang and Xu, 2010; Tran et al., 2017).

With increased focus on characters in creative documents like movies and fictional stories, the task of generating character descriptions using automatic summarization been proposed recently (Zhang et al., 2019). The accompanying dataset contains 1,036,965 fictional stories and 942,218 summaries.

While there has been prior work on summarizing short stories (Kazantseva, 2006), more recent methods in summarizing books utilize the hierarchical structure of documents for understanding the complex inter-dependencies in the text. Wu et al. (2021) incorporate human feedback along with recursive task decomposition, using summaries of small sections of the book to produce an overall summary at inference time. Pang et al. (2022) propose a novel top-down and bottom-up inference framework, which is effective on a variety of long document summarization benchmarks, including books.

5 Discussion

This workshop proposes the task of summarizing documents containing creative textual content. We consider sub-tasks focusing on the summarization of book chapters, movie scripts and transcripts from TV shows. Each sub-task highlights key challenges in automatic summarization of creative texts in a different genre. We also discuss how other efforts in the literature have attempted to approach this area of research. In its first version as part of COLING 2022, our sub-tasks attracted 18 submissions in total. We present the results from these submissions, along with some baselines and compare the performance of the different systems.

Summarization of creative texts opens the door for the development of computer-based tools to aid authors and marketers in creative industries (Toubia, 2021). Automatic summaries can serve as an important component of screenwriting and book-writing tools, helping grade the quality and gauge interest amongst the consumers (Gorinski and Lapata, 2015).

Advances in Creative Summarization will also assist and augment research in other related tasks and areas. Cues from textual summaries and automated content analysis in movie scripts can be helpful in creating movie-image summaries (Tsoneva et al., 2007).

There are two main directions to improve efforts in this direction in the future - incorporating more datasets/sub-tasks that relate to creative summarization, and improving metrics/strategies to effectively evaluate these systems. Other sources on the web, such as the one used by Zhang et al. (2019) can be used for harnessing datasets for summarizing creative texts. Similarly, our evaluation scheme can be expanded to include more entity-centric metrics (Chen et al., 2021), which can be crucial for identifying the presence of key characters in summaries of creative texts.

References

Marta Aparício, Paulo Figueiredo, Francisco Raposo, David Martins de Matos, Ricardo Ribeiro, and Luís Marujo. 2016. Summarization of films and documentaries based on subtitles and scripts. *Pattern Recognition Letters*, 73:7–12.

Iz Beltagy, Matthew E Peters, and Arman Cohan. 2020. Longformer: The long-document transformer. *arXiv preprint arXiv:2004.05150*.

Mingda Chen, Zewei Chu, Sam Wiseman, and Kevin Gimpel. 2021. Summscreen: A dataset for abstractive screenplay summarization. *arXiv preprint arXiv:2104.07091*.

Mingda Chen and Kevin Gimpel. 2021. Tvrecap: A dataset for generating stories with character descriptions. *arXiv preprint arXiv:2109.08833*.

Philip Gorinski and Mirella Lapata. 2015. Movie script summarization as graph-based scene extraction. In *Proceedings of the 2015 Conference of the North American Chapter of the Association for Computational Linguistics: Human Language Technologies*, pages 1066–1076.

Max Grusky, Mor Naaman, and Yoav Artzi. 2018. Newsroom: A dataset of 1.3 million summaries with diverse extractive strategies. In *Proceedings of the 2018 Conference of the North American Chapter of the Association for Computational Linguistics: Human Language Technologies, Volume 1 (Long Papers)*, pages 708–719, New Orleans, Louisiana. Association for Computational Linguistics.

Anna Kazantseva. 2006. An approach to summarizing short stories. In *Student Research Workshop*, pages 55–62.

Wojciech Kryscinski, Nazneen Fatema Rajani, Divyansh Agarwal, Caiming Xiong, and Dragomir R Radev. 2021. Booksum: A collection of datasets for long-form narrative summarization.

Philippe Laban, Tobias Schnabel, Paul N. Bennett, and Marti A. Hearst. 2022. SummaC: Re-visiting NLI-based models for inconsistency detection in summarization. *Transactions of the Association for Computational Linguistics*, 10:163–177.

Faisal Ladhak, Esin Durmus, He He, Claire Cardie, and Kathleen McKeown. 2022. Faithful or extractive? on mitigating the faithfulness-abstractiveness trade-off in abstractive summarization. In *Proceedings of the 60th Annual Meeting of the Association for Computational Linguistics (Volume 1: Long Papers)*, pages 1410–1421, Dublin, Ireland. Association for Computational Linguistics.

Faisal Ladhak, Bryan Li, Yaser Al-Onaizan, and Kathleen R. McKeown. 2020. Exploring content selection in summarization of novel chapters. In *Proceedings of the 58th Annual Meeting of the Association for Computational Linguistics, ACL 2020, Online, July 5-10, 2020*, pages 5043–5054. Association for Computational Linguistics.

Chin-Yew Lin. 2004. ROUGE: A package for automatic evaluation of summaries. In *Text Summarization Branches Out*, pages 74–81, Barcelona, Spain. Association for Computational Linguistics.

Rada Mihalcea and Hakan Ceylan. 2007. Explorations in automatic book summarization. In *EMNLP-CoNLL 2007, Proceedings of the 2007 Joint Conference on Empirical Methods in Natural Language Processing and Computational Natural Language Learning, June 28-30, 2007, Prague, Czech Republic*, pages 380–389. ACL.

Ani Nenkova, Julia Hirschberg, and Yang Liu, editors. 2011. *Proceedings of the Workshop on Automatic Summarization for Different Genres, Media, and Languages*. Association for Computational Linguistics, Portland, Oregon.

Bo Pang, Erik Nijkamp, Wojciech Kryściński, Silvio Savarese, Yingbo Zhou, and Caiming Xiong. 2022. Long document summarization with top-down and bottom-up inference. *arXiv preprint arXiv:2203.07586*.

Jitao Sang and Changsheng Xu. 2010. Character-based movie summarization. In *Proceedings of the 18th ACM international conference on Multimedia*, pages 855–858.

Tal Schuster, Adam Fisch, and Regina Barzilay. 2021. Get your vitamin C! robust fact verification with contrastive evidence. In *Proceedings of the 2021 Conference of the North American Chapter of the Association for Computational Linguistics: Human Language Technologies*, pages 624–643, Online. Association for Computational Linguistics.

Uri Shaham, Elad Segal, Maor Ivgi, Avia Efrat, Ori Yoran, Adi Haviv, Ankit Gupta, Wenhan Xiong, Mor Geva, Jonathan Berant, et al. 2022. Scrolls: Standardized comparison over long language sequences. *arXiv preprint arXiv:2201.03533*.

TAC. 2008. *Proceedings of the First Text Analysis Conference, TAC 2008, Gaithersburg, Maryland, USA, November 17-19, 2008*. NIST.

Olivier Toubia. 2017. The summarization of creative content. *Columbia Business School Research Paper*, (17-86).

Olivier Toubia. 2021. A poisson factorization topic model for the study of creative documents (and their summaries). *Journal of Marketing Research*, 58(6):1142–1158.

Quang Dieu Tran, Dosam Hwang, O Lee, Jai E Jung, et al. 2017. Exploiting character networks for movie summarization. *Multimedia Tools and Applications*, 76(8):10357–10369.

Tsvetomira Tsoneva, Mauro Barbieri, and Hans Weda. 2007. Automated summarization of narrative video on a semantic level. In *International conference on semantic computing (ICSC 2007)*, pages 169–176. IEEE.

Jeff Wu, Long Ouyang, Daniel M Ziegler, Nisan Stiennon, Ryan Lowe, Jan Leike, and Paul Christiano. 2021. Recursively summarizing books with human feedback. *arXiv preprint arXiv:2109.10862*.

Shiyue Zhang and Mohit Bansal. 2021. Finding a balanced degree of automation for summary evaluation. In *Proceedings of the 2021 Conference on Empirical Methods in Natural Language Processing*, pages 6617–6632, Online and Punta Cana, Dominican Republic. Association for Computational Linguistics.

Tianyi Zhang, Varsha Kishore, Felix Wu, Kilian Q. Weinberger, and Yoav Artzi. 2020. Bertscore: Evaluating text generation with BERT. In *8th International Conference on Learning Representations, ICLR 2020, Addis Ababa, Ethiopia, April 26-30, 2020*. OpenReview.net.

Weiwei Zhang, Jackie Chi Kit Cheung, and Joel Oren. 2019. Generating character descriptions for automatic summarization of fiction. In *Proceedings of the AAAI Conference on Artificial Intelligence*, volume 33, pages 7476–7483.

A Shared Task Submissions

The evaluation results for all the submissions to the sub-tasks are presented below in Tables 2-5. We use the original name of the system outputs as submitted by the participants to identify each submission.

Models	R_{1f}	R_{2f}	R_{Lf}	BS_P	BS_R	BS_{F1}	LP_{p3c}	SummaC$_{ZS}$	Length	Density	Coverage	1-grams	2-grams
Baselines													
LED_{1024}	0.1413	0.0214	0.1329	0.4318	0.4697	0.4446	0.2684	0.2599	937	1.5149	0.7230	0.2886	0.7094
LED_{4096}	0.1537	0.0221	0.1426	0.4232	0.4727	0.4420	0.2642	0.4718	866	2.9900	0.7617	0.2409	0.6096
LED_{16384}	0.1487	0.0218	0.1385	0.4282	0.4928	0.4544	0.2221	0.4132	755	2.2112	0.7372	0.2532	0.6541
Sub-Task 1 submissions													
MHPK	0.2975	0.0789	0.2833	0.5303	0.5553	0.5410	0.1071	0.1562	1465	2.1802	0.7735	0.3055	0.6775
LRL_NC	0.2643	0.0471	0.2436	0.4717	0.5264	0.4955	0.0669	0.3499	3345	12.6336	0.8336	0.1600	0.3457

Table 2: Sub-task 1 results for the baselines and the submissions on the *BookSumm-chapters* dataset.

Models	R_{1f}	R_{2f}	R_{Lf}	BS_P	BS_R	BS_{F1}	LP_{p3c}	SummaC$_{ZS}$	Length	Density	Coverage	1-grams	2-grams
Baselines													
LED_{1024}	0.1492	0.0146	0.1373	0.4298	0.4238	0.4258	0.2517	0.0000	903	1.1809	0.7021	0.3357	0.7485
LED_{4096}	0.1416	0.0130	0.1299	0.4245	0.4137	0.4179	0.2674	0.0000	877	1.3432	0.7311	0.3092	0.7273
LED_{16384}	0.1368	0.0125	0.1277	0.4322	0.3924	0.4099	0.2312	0.0000	551	1.4103	0.7266	0.3024	0.7211
Sub-Task 2 submissions													
MovING_scriptbase	0.4144	0.0823	0.3963	0.5163	0.5233	0.5194	0.0356	0.0476	729	3.4398	0.8759	0.1621	0.4827
UdS_scriptbase	0.4285	0.1088	0.4125	0.5543	0.5410	0.5474	0.0587	0.0323	883	1.3489	0.7778	0.2911	0.7346
UdS_base_bs4_0.2noisy	0.4634	0.1158	0.4405	0.5723	0.5680	0.5700	0.0372	0.0250	791	1.2722	0.7502	0.3520	0.7636
UdS_base_bs4_Bitfit	0.4344	0.1091	0.4178	0.5533	0.5402	0.5465	0.0566	0.0321	815	1.3475	0.7753	0.2879	0.7301
UdS_base_bs4_Bitfit_Mix01	0.4580	0.1162	0.4376	0.5664	0.5601	0.5631	0.0459	0.0316	770	1.3226	0.7590	0.3235	0.7457
UdS_base_bs4_Bitfit_Mix10	0.4576	0.1158	0.4380	0.5690	0.5620	0.5653	0.0418	0.0301	781	1.3194	0.7628	0.3167	0.7459
UdS_base_bs4	0.4639	0.1152	0.4408	0.5703	0.5672	0.5686	0.0408	0.0269	780	1.2733	0.7513	0.3456	0.7604
UdS_base_bs5_Bitfit	0.4316	0.1088	0.4151	0.5542	0.5414	0.5475	0.0567	0.0309	838	1.3451	0.7774	0.2890	0.7327
UdS_base_bs5_Bitfit_Mix01	0.4550	0.1149	0.4344	0.5664	0.5606	0.5634	0.0508	0.0322	776	1.3344	0.7621	0.3205	0.7438
UdS_base_bs5_Bitfit_Mix10	0.4553	0.1146	0.4353	0.5677	0.5619	0.5646	0.0435	0.0295	777	1.3235	0.7596	0.3218	0.7462
UdS_base_bs5	0.4604	0.1140	0.4369	0.5699	0.5668	0.5682	0.0410	0.0281	783	1.2709	0.7493	0.3485	0.7649

Table 3: Sub-task 2 results for the baselines and the submissions on the *Scriptbase* dataset.

Models	R_{1f}	R_{2f}	R_{Lf}	BS_P	BS_R	BS_{F1}	LP_{p3c}	SummaC$_{ZS}$	Length	Density	Coverage	1-grams	2-grams
Baselines													
LED_{1024}	0.1428	0.0154	0.1236	0.4100	0.4107	0.4052	0.0987	0.0559	330	1.1440	0.7148	0.3060	0.7801
LED_{4096}	0.1694	0.0209	0.1501	0.4591	0.4752	0.4600	0.0304	0.1052	188	1.4378	0.7343	0.2803	0.7314
LED_{16384}	0.1514	0.0170	0.1334	0.4485	0.4632	0.4489	0.0304	0.1644	192	1.5474	0.7108	0.2904	0.7285
Sub-Task 3 submissions													
inotum	0.2860	0.0624	0.2529	0.5934	0.5609	0.5750	0.0559	0.0272	86	1.0321	0.6664	0.3715	0.8251
team_ufal	0.2469	0.0408	0.2300	0.5038	0.5590	0.5285	0.0406	0.1282	289	2.0821	0.7127	0.2484	0.6498
AMRTVSumm	0.2307	0.0303	0.2106	0.4906	0.5344	0.5108	0.0138	0.024	256	0.8789	0.6137	0.4924	0.8569

Table 4: Sub-task 3 results for the baselines and the submissions on the *SummScreenFD* dataset.

Models	R_{1f}	R_{2f}	R_{Lf}	BS_P	BS_R	BS_{F1}	LP_{p3c}	SummaC$_{ZS}$	Length	Density	Coverage	1-grams	2-grams
Baselines													
LED_{1024}	0.0727	0.0063	0.0652	0.4100	0.4107	0.4052	0.0304	0.0905	984	0.9530	0.6302	0.3781	0.8379
LED_{4096}	0.0822	0.0062	0.0753	0.4122	0.4086	0.4057	0.0304	0.0837	879	0.8457	0.5822	0.4091	0.8674
LED_{16384}	0.0722	0.0047	0.0656	0.4096	0.3916	0.3960	0.0304	0.0800	885	0.7544	0.5430	0.4387	0.8931
Sub-Task 4 submissions													
AdityaUpadhyay	0.3921	0.0909	0.3794	0.5507	0.5550	0.5516	0.0625	0.1133	316	1.9436	0.7618	0.2026	0.6688
AMRTVSumm	0.3426	0.0717	0.328	0.5385	0.5318	0.5347	0.0152	0.0499	259	1.1024	0.7291	0.3514	0.7931

Table 5: Sub-task 4 results for the baselines and the submissions on the *SummScreenTMS* dataset.

Author Index

Agarwal, Divyansh, 67
Agarwal, Raksha, 13

Bae, Suyoung, 51
Bhatnagar, Aakash, 44
Bhavsar, Nidhir, 44

Chang, Ernie, 57
Chatterjee, Niladri, 13
Cheong, Yun-Gyung, 51
Cho, Gunhee, 51

Demberg, Vera, 57
Deng, Zhaoyuan, 36

Eder, Tobias, 29

Fabbri, Alexander R., 67

Groh, Georg, 29

Han, Simeng, 67
Hong, Xudong, 57
Hua, Yilun, 36

Kashyap, Prerna, 19
Kees, Nataliia, 29
Khatri, Aadyant, 13
Kim, Eunchong, 51
Kryscinski, Wojciech, 67
Kumar, Rishu, 24

Ladhak, Faisal, 67
Li, Bryan, 67
Lin, Pin-Jie, 57

McKeown, Kathleen, 67
Middleton, Stuart E., 1
Millard, David E., 1
Motlicek, Petr, 44

Nguyen, Thien, 29

Pu, Dongqi, 57

Radev, Dragomir, 67
Revi, Ashwathy T., 1

Rosa, Rudolf, 24

Singh, Muskaan, 44

Upadhyay, Aditya, 44

Wiseman, Sam, 67

Xu, Zhijie, 36

Yoo, Taewoo, 51

Zhang, Tianyi, 67

Association for Computational Linguistics
209 N. Eighth Street
Stroudsburg, Pennsylvania 18360

ISBN 978-1-7138-9106-2

CURRAN ASSOCIATES INC.
proceedings.com

First Workshop on Natural Language Processing for Human Resources (NLP4HR 2024)

St. Julian's, Malta
22 March 2024